AF496771

Harvesting Nature's Silent Symphony

Harvesting Nature's Silent Symphony

Sam Loray

Mohammed Altaf Hussain

CONTENTS

5.1 Explore the environmental factors that influence nature's symphony, such as climate, geography, and topography.

5.2 Discuss the delicate balance and the impact of human activities on the environment.

5.3 Emphasize the need for sustainable practices to preserve the symphony.

Chapter 6: The Harmony of Water

6.1 Investigate the role of water bodies in shaping the symphony of nature.

6.2 Discuss the importance of rivers, lakes, and oceans in supporting life.

6.3 Explore the impact of human activities on water ecosystems and conservation efforts.

Chapter 7: The Song of the Sky - Birds and Beyond

7.1 Focus on the avian contributions to the silent symphony.

7.2 Explore the migration patterns, nesting behaviors, and calls of birds.

7.3 Discuss the role of the atmosphere and celestial bodies in the symphonic narrative.

Chapter 8: Crescendo of Conservation

8.1 Examine the current state of environmental conservation efforts globally.

8.2 Discuss success stories and challenges in preserving biodiversity.

8.3 Encourage readers to actively participate in conservation and sustainable practices.

Chapter 9: Coda - A Call to Action

9.1 Summarize the key lessons learned from the exploration of nature's silent symphony.

9.2 Inspire readers to appreciate, respect, and actively contribute to preserving the delicate balance of the natural world.

9.3 Provide practical steps and resources for individuals to engage in conservation efforts.

Introduction

In the quietude of the regular world, where the stir of leaves and the delicate mumble of a stream make an ensemble that frequently slips by everyone's notice, lies a significant and perplexing embroidery of life. This orchestra is made not out of notes and tunes, but rather of the horde sounds, sights, and rhythms that radiate from the unpredictable dance of widely varied vegetation. It is a quiet ensemble, directed naturally itself, working out in the immense scenes, thick timberlands, and extensive seas that make up our planet.

As people, we have for quite some time been charmed by the marvels of the regular world. From the earliest human advancements to the current day, our relationship with nature has been both mind boggling and cooperative. We have drawn motivation from its excellence, looked for comfort in its serenity, and outfit its assets for food and endurance. However, in the midst of the buzzing about of present day life, the amicable orchestra of nature frequently blurs out of spotlight, muffled by the chaos of metropolitan living.

The demonstration of gathering nature's quiet ensemble is a figurative excursion that rises above the simple extraction of assets. It is a call to rediscover the significant interconnectedness among humankind and the regular world, to check out the inconspicuous tunes that reverberation through environments, and to see the value in the fragile equilibrium that supports life on The planet. This ensemble incorporates not just the perceptible components that arrive at our ears yet additionally the concealed strings that wind around together the complicated trap of biodiversity and biological flexibility.

At the core of this ensemble is the dance of life itself - an expressive dance of animal groups, each assuming a novel part in the terrific story of presence. The vegetation, with their photosynthetic ability, make the very air we inhale, while the fauna, from the littlest bugs to the biggest warm blooded creatures, add to the rich biodiversity that characterizes our planet. The perplexing connections among hunters and prey, pollinators and blossoms, and cooperative organizations that range biological systems are the notes and harmonies that structure the arrangement of nature's quiet ensemble.

However, as we wonder about the magnificence and intricacy of this ensemble, we should likewise stand up to the difficulties that take steps to disturb its sensitive equilibrium. Human exercises, driven by a developing populace and a voracious interest for assets, have prompted deforestation, living space obliteration, and the consumption of biodiversity. The results of environmental change pose a potential threat, creating a shaded area over the steadiness of biological systems and the fate of endless species.

Chasing progress, we have in some cases failed to remember that we are nevertheless one piece of the bigger group of life on The planet. The outcomes of this oversight are turning out to be progressively clear, as environments face extraordinary difficulties and species waver near the very edge of elimination. The dire need to reexamine our relationship with nature has never been more clear, and the similitude of collecting nature's quiet ensemble takes on a strong importance.

Reaping, with regards to this ensemble, is certainly not an uneven extraction of assets for human advantage yet a nuanced and corresponding connection with nature. It includes perceiving the intrinsic worth of biodiversity, understanding the environmental administrations that biological systems give, and encouraging a feeling of stewardship that rises above ages. It is tied in with receiving the rewards of nature's abundance mindfully, with a consciousness of the many-sided associations that support life.

The quiet ensemble of nature stretches out past the earthbound domains to the tremendous regions of seas and streams that support our planet. The musical lapping of waves, the eerie calls of marine animals, and the lively tints of coral reefs make an orchestra underneath the surface that is essentially as dazzling as the one ashore. However, the seas, once accepted to be unfathomable in their ability to assimilate human effects, presently bear the scars of overfishing, contamination, and environmental change.

As we explore the difficulties of the Anthropocene, there is a developing acknowledgment that the soundness of the seas is complicatedly connected to the prosperity of the whole planet. The demonstration of gathering nature's quiet orchestra should reach out to the watery profundities, where economical fisheries, marine preservation, and the insurance of basic biological systems become basic. The ensemble of the seas, similar to its earthly partner, requires an amicable cooperation among mankind and the normal world.

In the woven artwork of nature, native networks arise as key caretakers of customary information and supportable practices. Their close association with the land, went down through ages, offers significant experiences into living together as one with nature. The demonstration of collecting nature's quiet orchestra turns into a cooperative exertion, where native insight joins with current logical comprehension to fashion a way toward a more maintainable future.

Nonetheless, the excursion towards agreeable concurrence with nature is full of difficulties, both foundational and person. The globalized idea of asset extraction, driven by financial goals, frequently prompts double-dealing and corruption of environments. Adjusting the requirement for financial improvement with natural maintainability requires a change in perspective in our way to deal with asset the board and preservation.

Individual decisions likewise assume a significant part in the ensemble of nature. From buyer choices that impact interest for unreasonable items to way of life decisions that add to carbon impressions, every individual turns into a member in the continuous creation of the quiet ensemble. Mindfulness and instruction become impetuses for change, engaging people to settle on informed decisions that line up with the standards of manageability.

Chasing reaping nature's quiet ensemble, innovation arises as both a test and an open door. Propels in science and development offer new apparatuses for checking biological systems, figuring out biodiversity, and executing preservation measures. However, the very innovative progressions that work with asset extraction and modern cycles likewise present dangers to the sensitive equilibrium of nature. Finding some kind of harmony between innovative advancement and biological protection turns into a critical part of the ensemble's piece.

The idea of gathering nature's quiet ensemble stretches out past the domains of environment and preservation to envelop the domains of craftsmanship, culture, and otherworldliness. All through mankind's set of experiences, nature has been a wellspring of motivation for craftsmen, writers, and masterminds. The quiet ensemble, with its complex songs and immortal rhythms, turns into a dream for innovative articulation, inciting reflection on the magnificence and delicacy of the normal world.

In the otherworldly aspects, the demonstration of reaping nature's quiet ensemble takes on an extraordinary quality. It includes a profound worship for the interconnected trap of life, an affirmation of the holiness intrinsic in nature, and an acknowledgment of our job as stewards of the Earth. Otherworldly customs from different societies all over the planet offer bits of knowledge into the significant association among mankind and the normal world, highlighting the significance of living together as one with the rhythms of creation.

As we set out on the excursion of collecting nature's quiet ensemble, obviously the errand isn't simply about safeguarding business as usual yet about embracing the dynamism innate in biological systems. Nature is tough, and offered the chance, it can recover and flourish. Rebuilding and rewilding become indispensable parts of the orchestra, permitting environments to recuperate and recover, encouraging a recharged feeling of expectation for what's in store.

Chapter 1

Prelude to the Symphony

In the tremendous territory of the universe, where systems spin in a vast artful dance and stars murmur together as one, there exists an ensemble that originates before the beginning of mankind. This grandiose suggestion, unfurling across the enormous material, makes way for the multifaceted dance of life on a small blue planet settled in the vast immensity. This ensemble is a preface, an infinite preamble to the stupendous story of presence.

As we look at the night sky, we are seeing the reverberations of this grandiose orchestra, an immortal structure that started billions of years prior. The birth and demise of stars, the disastrous occasions that shape worlds, and the ages long excursion of infinite residue are all essential for this divine suggestion. It is an orchestra of creation and obliteration, a grandiose expressive dance that rises above the limits of reality.

On The planet, our story starts against the scenery of this enormous introduction. The unrefined components of life, fashioned in the blazing heaters of far off stars, blend into the early stage soup that brings forth the main stirrings of life. The orchestra of advancement becomes the dominant focal point, with the gradual rise of basic creatures that ultimately develop into the assorted cluster of life shapes that populate the planet today.

The preface to the orchestra is a story written in the language of DNA, a hereditary code that conveys the guidelines for life's complicated dance. From single-celled creatures to complex multicellular life, the ensemble of development coordinates the rise of different species, each assuming an exceptional part in the unfurling show of life. It is a story of variation, endurance, and the tireless quest for presence notwithstanding consistently evolving conditions.

As life develops, the orchestra expands its venture into the domains of nature and biological systems. The connections between species, the sensitive harmony between hunter and prey, and the reliance of verdure become the notes and harmonies of an agreeable organization. The introduction to the ensemble is a festival of biodiversity, an indication of the multifaceted associations that wind around together the embroidery of life on The planet.

The development of mankind denotes a crescendo in the orchestra, as cognizance and mindfulness become basic parts of the story. People, enriched with the limit with respect to reason and reflection, assume the job of stewards in the amazing arrangement of the normal world. The preface to the orchestra turns into a call to liability, an update that our activities resonate through the perplexing snare of life.

However, with the coming of human development, the orchestra experiences disharmony. The quest for progress, driven by mechanical development and industrialization, acquaints another dynamic with the regular world. The preface to the orchestra observes the ascent of farming, the forming of scenes, and the double-dealing of regular assets on a remarkable scale. The human impression turns into a permanent blemish on the World's surface, changing biological systems and setting off an influx of eliminations.

Directly following this human-driven discord, the introduction to the ensemble takes on a solemn tone. The outcomes of deforestation, contamination, and over-exploitation cast a shadow over the amicable coordination of nature. The sensitive equilibrium that supported life for ages is undermined, and the orchestra faces an emergency that requests consideration, reflection, and purposeful endeavors to reestablish harmony.

In the cutting edge time, the preface to the ensemble unfurls against the background of the Anthropocene - an age characterized by the significant effect of human exercises in the world. Environmental change, driven by the arrival of ozone depleting substances, arises as a focal subject in the unfurling story.

The ensemble wrestles with climbing temperatures, softening ice covers, and the interruption of weather conditions, flagging a planetary-scale challenge that rises above lines and limits.

In the midst of the difficulties of the Anthropocene, the preface to the orchestra turns into a mobilizing sob for natural stewardship and maintainable living. It requires an amicable concurrence among mankind and the regular world, where the quest for progress is offset with a profound regard for the complex snare of life. The orchestra entices us to reevaluate our relationship with the Earth, to pay attention to the murmurs of biological systems, and to graph a course towards a more manageable future.

The idea of gathering nature's quiet orchestra arises as a figurative excursion inside the bigger introduction to the ensemble. An illustration epitomizes the possibility of dependably captivating with the normal world, recognizing the natural worth of biodiversity, and cultivating a feeling of stewardship that reaches out across ages. Collecting, in this specific circumstance, turns into a nuanced and corresponding collaboration with nature, an approach to receiving the rewards of the World's abundance without undermining its fragile equilibrium.

The introduction to the ensemble expands its venture into the huge regions of seas, where marine biological systems reverberation the inestimable rhythms of life. The orchestra of the oceans, with its cadenced tides, dynamic coral reefs, and various marine life, faces extraordinary difficulties. Overfishing, plastic contamination, and the fermentation of seas compromise the sensitive equilibrium of marine environments, creating a shaded area over the introduction's sea developments.

As humankind wrestles with the ramifications of its activities, the introduction to the orchestra requests a reexamination of our relationship with the seas. Feasible fisheries, marine protection, and worldwide endeavors to decrease plastic waste become vital developments inside the oceanic developments of the ensemble. The amicable concurrence with the seas turns into a crucial part of the general story of the World's orchestra.

In the unpredictable transaction among mankind and nature, native networks arise as vital participants in the preface to the ensemble. Their customary information, went down through ages, offers important experiences into maintainable living and agreeable conjunction with the normal world. The orchestra becomes enhanced with the songs of native insight, as networks endeavor to safeguard their genealogical grounds and protect the biodiversity that supports them.

However, the orchestra experiences obstructions on the worldwide stage. The foundational difficulties of asset extraction, driven by financial goals, frequently lead to the double-dealing of normal assets and natural corruption. The preface to the ensemble turns into a landmark where the powers of protection and double-dealing conflict, requesting a reconsideration of cultural qualities and needs.

Individual decisions arise as pivotal developments inside the introduction to the ensemble. The day to day choices made by people, from customer decisions to way of life propensities, shape the story of the orchestra. Mindfulness and training become impetuses for change, engaging people to settle on decisions that line up with the standards of manageability. The orchestra, in its preface, requires an aggregate arousing, encouraging every individual to turn into a careful member in the continuous creation of the World's story.

Innovation, with its double nature, becomes both a test and an open door inside the preface to the orchestra. Progresses in science and development offer new apparatuses for checking biological systems, figuring out biodiversity, and carrying out protection measures. Nonetheless, the very mechanical headways that work with asset extraction and modern cycles additionally present dangers to the fragile equilibrium of nature. Finding some kind of harmony between mechanical advancement and biological safeguarding turns into a vital development inside the ensemble.

The preface to the orchestra expands its ringlets into the domains of craftsmanship, culture, and otherworldliness. All through mankind's set of experiences, nature has been a wellspring of motivation for specialists, writers, and scholars. The orchestra, with its mind boggling songs and immortal rhythms, turns into a dream for inventive articulation, inciting reflection on the magnificence and delicacy of the normal world. In the otherworldly aspects, the preface to the ensemble takes on an extraordinary quality, including a profound worship for the interconnected snare of life and an acknowledgment of the holiness intrinsic in nature.

As we stand at the edge of the orchestra, the preface requires a recharged obligation to natural preservation and feasible living. It is a challenge to pay attention to the orchestra of nature, to adjust our faculties to the unpretentious songs that reverberation through environments, and to perceive the significant interconnectedness among humankind and the normal world. The introduction to the ensemble is an update that, as stewards of the Earth, we have the obligation to support and safeguard the fragile equilibrium that supports life on this phenomenal planet.

All in all, the preface to the ensemble is an investigation of the vast beginnings of life, the transformative excursion of species, and the complicated exchange among humankind and nature. It makes way for the figurative excursion of reaping nature's quiet ensemble, an excursion that includes dependable commitment with the regular world, a profound regard for biodiversity, and a guarantee to practical living. As we leave on this excursion, the introduction to the orchestra resounds as an immortal story that calls for concordance, balance, and an aggregate work to guarantee the kept prospering of life on The planet.

1.1 Introduction to the concept of nature's silent symphony.

In the multifaceted embroidery of our planet, nature organizes an orchestra that rises above human comprehension. An ensemble unfurls in the stir of leaves, the chattering of streams, and the amicable dance of biological systems.

This orchestra, nonetheless, isn't perceptible in the ordinary sense; it is a quiet sythesis, resounding through the fragile equilibrium of the regular world. This idea, appropriately named "Nature's Quiet Ensemble," exemplifies the complicated inter-action of biological cycles, biodiversity, and the interconnected snare of life on The planet.

At its center, Nature's Quiet Ensemble is a figurative articulation that welcomes us to pay attention to the inconspicuous subtleties of the regular world. It provokes us to adjust our faculties to the many-sided rhythms and songs that exude from the bio-logical systems that encompass us. Dissimilar to a customary ensemble with noticeable melodic notes, this quiet orchestra is made out of the horde communications between species, the progressions of energy, and the repeating examples of life and passing. An ensemble works out in the immense regions of timberlands, the profundities of seas, and the mosaic of scenes that characterize our planet.

The quiet idea of this ensemble doesn't reduce its importance; rather, it highlights that the most significant parts of nature frequently work past the domain of human discernment. It coaxes us to perceive that the strength of environments, the variety of species, and the versatility of the regular world add to an orchestra that, while quiet to our ears, is fundamental for the food of life.

As we dig into the layers of Nature's Quiet Ensemble, it becomes obvious that the idea isn't restricted to a particular area or biological system. All things considered, a widespread subject envelops earthly and oceanic domains, from the profundities of rainforests to the endlessness of deserts. The quiet orchestra reaches out to the seas, where the recurring pattern of tides, the dynamic tints of coral reefs, and the multifaceted dance of marine life make a watery sonata that reflects the intricacy of life ashore.

To get a handle on the pith of Nature's Quiet Orchestra, perceiving the interconnectedness of all living things is fundamental. Every species, from the littlest microorganisms to the biggest vertebrates, assumes a novel part in the orchestra. The hunters and prey, the pollinators and plants, and the bunch collaborations that characterize environmental connections add to the piece of this quiet show-stopper. The expulsion or adjustment of any component inside this multifaceted web can disturb the amicable equilibrium and modify the tune of the ensemble.

With regards to Nature's Quiet Ensemble, the demonstration of "gathering" takes on a nuanced meaning. It's anything but a straightforward extraction of assets for human increase yet a figurative and complementary cooperation with nature. Reaping, in this sense, includes recognizing the characteristic worth of biodiversity, understanding the biological administrations that environments give, and encouraging a feeling of stewardship that rises above ages. It is tied in with receiving the rewards of nature mindfully, with an attention to the sensitive equilibrium that supports life.

As we investigate the idea further, it is vital to consider the difficulties that Nature's Quiet Orchestra faces in the advanced period. Human exercises, driven by populace development and asset requests, have prompted deforestation, environment annihilation, and the exhaustion of biodiversity. Environmental change, energized by the arrival of ozone depleting substances, represents a danger to the security of biological systems and the endurance of incalculable species. The quiet ensemble, once versatile and persevering, presently fights with the problematic powers of anthropogenic effect.

The desperation to reexamine our relationship with nature turns out to be progressively obvious notwithstanding these difficulties. Nature's Quiet Ensemble turns into a figurative source of inspiration, encouraging humankind to tune in, comprehend, and blend with the regular world. It energizes a change in context from review nature as an asset to be taken advantage of to remembering it as a fragile and interconnected framework that requires cautious stewardship.

The quiet ensemble broadens its rings into the tremendous breadths of seas, where marine environments face their own arrangement of difficulties. Overfishing, plastic contamination, and the fermentation of seas compromise the fragile equilibrium of marine life. The ensemble of the oceans, once overflowing with life and imperativeness, presently experiences harsh notes that reverberation the effect of human exercises. The figurative demonstration of gathering nature's quiet orchestra requires a reexamination of our relationship with the seas, stressing economical practices and preservation measures.

Native people group arise as key overseers of conventional information and maintainable practices inside the account of Nature's Quiet Orchestra. Their close association with the land, went down through ages, offers important experiences into living together as one with nature. The quiet orchestra becomes improved with the songs of native insight, as networks endeavor to safeguard their familial grounds and save the biodiversity that supports them.

Be that as it may, the agreeable story of Nature's Quiet Orchestra experiences fundamental difficulties. The globalized idea of asset extraction, driven by financial goals, frequently prompts double-dealing and corruption of environments. The fragile equilibrium of the ensemble is undermined by the tenacious quest for benefit without due thought for the drawn out results.

Individual decisions arise as vital developments inside Nature's Quiet Orchestra. The choices made by people, from purchaser decisions to way of life propensities, shape the account of the ensemble. Mindfulness and training become impetuses for change, enabling people to settle on decisions that line up with the standards of supportability. The quiet orchestra, in its figurative embodiment, requires an aggregate arousing, encouraging every individual to turn into a careful member in the continuous structure of the World's story.

Innovation, with its double nature, becomes both a test and an open door inside the setting of Nature's Quiet Ensemble. Progresses in science and advancement offer new apparatuses for observing environments, figuring out biodiversity, and carrying out preservation measures. In any case, the very mechanical progressions that work with asset extraction and modern cycles likewise present dangers to the sensitive equilibrium of nature. Finding some kind of harmony between innovative advancement and biological safeguarding turns into a significant development inside the ensemble.

The quiet orchestra expands its impact into the domains of craftsmanship, culture, and otherworldliness. All through mankind's set of experiences, nature has been a wellspring of motivation for specialists, writers, and masterminds. The orchestra, with its many-sided songs and immortal rhythms, turns into a dream for innovative articulation, inciting reflection on the magnificence and delicacy of the regular world. In the otherworldly aspects, Nature's Quiet Ensemble takes on an extraordinary quality, including a profound veneration for the interconnected snare of life and an acknowledgment of the holiness inborn in nature.

As we set out on the excursion of Nature's Quiet Orchestra, obviously the errand isn't just about safeguarding the norm yet about embracing the dynamism inborn in biological systems. Nature is tough, and offered the chance, it can recover and flourish. Rebuilding and rewilding become essential parts of the ensemble, permitting environments to mend and recover, cultivating a recharged feeling of expectation for what's in store.

All in all, the prologue to the idea of Nature's Quiet Orchestra fills in as a door into a figurative and multi-layered investigation of humankind's relationship with the regular world. It makes way for a more profound comprehension of the inter-connected trap of life, the difficulties looked by biological systems, and the basic for mindful stewardship. Nature's Quiet Orchestra entices us to tune in, learn, and blend with the quiet yet significant songs of the World's perplexing story.

1.2 Explore the interconnectedness of ecosystems and the harmonious balance in nature.

The complicated dance of life on Earth unfurls inside the interconnected em-broidery of biological systems, each assuming a remarkable part in keeping up with the sensitive equilibrium of nature. Biological systems, characterized as powerful connections between living organic entities and their current circumstance, structure the underpinning of the planet's biodiversity and add to the general wellbeing and versatility of the normal world. To grasp the amicable equilibrium in nature, it is basic to dive into the significant interconnectedness of environments, perceiving how the strings of life wind around together in a perplexing and reliant web.

Biological systems, going from earthly woodlands to sea-going coral reefs, are portrayed by a variety of animal types that coincide and connect inside a particular geological region.

The vegetation, fauna, microorganisms, and abiotic factors inside an environment are complicatedly connected through an organization of connections, shaping a co-operative conjunction that supports life. This interconnectedness is the bedrock of the agreeable equilibrium saw in nature, where every component adds to the prosperity of the whole framework.

In earthbound environments, the connection among plants and creatures epito-mizes the interconnected dance of life. Plants, through the course of photosynthesis, bridle daylight to change over carbon dioxide into oxygen and sugars. This key inter-action supports vegetation as well as produces the oxygen fundamental for the breath of creatures. At the same time, creatures add to the biological system by partaking in fertilization, seed dispersal, and supplement spinning through their exercises.

The amicable equilibrium stretches out to the mind boggling hunter prey con-nections inside biological systems. Hunters assume a pivotal part in managing prey populaces, forestalling overgrazing and keeping up with the natural equilibrium. Alternately, prey species develop protection systems and versatile ways of behaving to escape predation, guaranteeing their endurance. This fragile dance among hunters and prey guarantees the solidness of biological systems, forestalling the uncontrolled multiplication or decline of explicit species.

The idea of trophic levels further highlights the interconnectedness of biological systems. In a trophic pyramid, energy streams from makers (plants) to essential shoppers (herbivores) and afterward to optional and tertiary customers (carnivores). Decomposers, like growths and microorganisms, make light of a fundamental job in breaking natural matter, reusing supplements once more into the environment. This energy move and supplement cycling inside trophic levels make an amicable equilibrium, forestalling asset consumption and guaranteeing the maintainability of life.

Sea-going environments, enveloping seas, lakes, and waterways, likewise embody the interconnectedness and agreeable equilibrium intrinsic in nature. Coral reefs, frequently alluded to as the "rainforests of the ocean," grandstand the cooperative connections between coral polyps and green growth. The corals give a safeguarded climate to the green growth, which, thus, give the corals fundamental supplements through photosynthesis. This mutualistic affiliation frames the groundwork of the lively and biodiverse environments tracked down in coral reefs.

In freshwater biological systems, the harmony between amphibian plants and herbivores, for example, fish, impacts water quality and supplement cycling. Oceanic plants ingest supplements from the water, adding to a better climate, while herbivores assist with controlling plant populaces, forestalling excess. This interconnected relationship guarantees the harmony of the biological system, encouraging circumstances reasonable for a different scope of sea-going life.

The interconnectedness of biological systems turns out to be much more clear while thinking about the idea of biomes - enormous geographic areas described by unambiguous environment, vegetation, and natural life. The World's biomes, including tropical rainforests, deserts, tundras, and fields, feature the versatility of life to different ecological circumstances. Relocation designs, occasional changes, and the many-sided connections between species add to the agreeable equilibrium inside every biome and the planet in general.

Past the noticeable communications between life forms, microorganisms assume a critical part in keeping up with the wellbeing of biological systems. Soil microorganisms, for example, add to supplement cycling, separating natural matter and working with the accessibility of fundamental components for plant development. The microbial local area in oceanic environments disintegrates natural material, sanitizing water and supporting the general equilibrium of the biological system.

The amicable equilibrium in nature isn't restricted to individual biological systems however stretches out across scenes and mainlands. Transitory species, like birds and vertebrates, cross immense distances, interfacing various environments and adding to the natural variety of different locales. These transient examples exhibit the consistent interconnectedness of environments on a worldwide scale, underlining the significance of saving different natural surroundings for the prosperity of transitory species.

Human exercises, nonetheless, have acquainted disturbances with the agreeable equilibrium of environments. Deforestation, contamination, environmental change, and natural surroundings obliteration present critical dangers to the interconnected snare of life. The deficiency of biodiversity, driven by human-actuated factors, upsets the unpredictable connections inside biological systems, prompting irregular characteristics that resonate across the regular world.

Environmental change, filled by the amassing of ozone harming substances in the climate, has broad ramifications for biological systems around the world. Adjusted atmospheric conditions, increasing temperatures, and outrageous occasions influence the dispersion and conduct of species. Coral fading, a peculiarity connected to environmental change, undermines the sensitive beneficial interaction between coral polyps and green growth, imperiling the wellbeing of coral reefs. The interconnectedness of biological systems implies that disturbances in a single region can have flowing impacts, enhancing the difficulties looked naturally.

The significance of protecting the interconnectedness and amicable equilibrium in nature is highlighted by the idea of environmental versatility. Biological systems with high strength can endure and recuperate from aggravations, keeping up with their fundamental capabilities and biodiversity. Protecting the interconnected snare of life upgrades the flexibility of environments, permitting them to adjust to changing circumstances and recuperate from outside pressures.

Preservation endeavors assume a critical part in protecting the agreeable equilibrium of biological systems. Safeguarded regions, natural life passageways, and reasonable land the board rehearses add to the conservation of biodiversity and the honesty of environments. Biological system based approaches, perceiving the interconnected idea of natural difficulties, intend to resolve issues comprehensively, taking into account the more extensive setting of environmental cooperations.

The acknowledgment of the interconnectedness of biological systems likewise requires a change in human points of view and practices. Taking on manageable ways of life, diminishing asset utilization, and advancing dependable land use are urgent moves toward sustaining the agreeable equilibrium of nature. Training and mindfulness drives assume an imperative part in cultivating a comprehension of the interconnected snare of life and the meaning of saving biodiversity for people in the future.

All in all, investigating the interconnectedness of biological systems discloses the multifaceted connections that structure the quiet ensemble of nature. The amicable equilibrium saw in nature is a demonstration of the complicated dance of life, where each specie, from the littlest microorganism to the biggest hunter, assumes an exceptional part. Perceiving and safeguarding the interconnected trap of life isn't just fundamental for the prosperity of individual environments but on the other hand is vital for the general wellbeing and maintainability of the planet. As stewards of the Earth, it is our obligation to stand by listening to the quiet orchestra, grasp its complicated tunes, and guarantee the coherence of the agreeable equilibrium that supports life on this phenomenal planet.

1.3 Setting the stage for the exploration of the various elements contributing to this symphony.

In the great performance center of the regular world, where the stage is set by the immense scenes, perplexing environments, and the horde life shapes that possess our planet, there unfurls a quiet ensemble - a structure that rises above human hear-able discernment however reverberates profoundly inside the multifaceted equilibrium of nature. Before we dive into the investigation of the different components adding to this quiet ensemble, it is fundamental for set the stage, to comprehend the overall setting where this many-sided organization of life happens.

The idea of Nature's Quiet Ensemble typifies the amicable connections, sensitive connections, and interconnected elements that characterize the living embroidery of Earth. A figurative articulation welcomes us to listen not with our ears but rather with our comprehension, to see the nuanced songs of biological systems, and to see the value in the quiet yet significant commitments of every component to the orchestra of life.

At the core of this ensemble lies biodiversity - the immense range of species that populate earthbound and sea-going domains. Biodiversity is the living sign of the ensemble, with every species assuming an unmistakable part in the piece.

From the minuscule organic entities that structure the groundwork of pecking orders to the appealling megafauna that catch our creative mind, each specie adds to the unpredictable songs of the quiet orchestra.

Biological systems, as the stage whereupon this orchestra unfurls, are complicated and dynamic networks of residing creatures interfacing with their current circumstance. From transcending woodlands to rambling fields, from coral reefs underneath the sea's surface to the tundra's frozen spread, biological systems make different environments that support and support life. The orchestra winds through these environments, with every one delivering special harmonies and rhythms, aggregately adding to the rich embroidered artwork of nature.

The patterns of life and passing are essential developments inside the ensemble, forming the rhythmic movement of energy through environments. Birth, development, proliferation, and rot are the phases of this unending cycle, where life forms assume their parts with accuracy. Decomposers, the uncelebrated yet truly great individuals of the orchestra, separate natural matter, returning supplements to the dirt and working with the restoration of life. This repetitive dance guarantees the manageability and versatility of biological systems.

Abiotic factors, the non-living parts of environments, give the scenery and structure to the orchestra. Soil, water, daylight, and environment are fundamental components that impact the dispersion and conduct of species. The accessibility of these abiotic factors decides the structure of biological systems and shapes the songs of the ensemble. Changes in environment, for instance, can adjust the beat and power of the ensemble, influencing the existence cycles and ways of behaving of species.

Hunter prey connections, a key part of the orchestra, present elements that control populaces and keep up with biological equilibrium. Hunters, in their quest for prey, forestall overpopulation and guarantee the soundness of environments. Prey species, thusly, foster techniques for endurance, making a sensitive dance of transformation and conjunction. These connections add to the strength and flexibility of environments, forestalling the predominance of any single species.

Relocation designs, one more development inside the orchestra, interface environments across landmasses and locales. Birds, vertebrates, and even bugs navigate huge distances, adding to the trading of hereditary material, working with fertilization, and affecting the biodiversity of different environments. Movement highlights the worldwide interconnectedness of nature, underlining that the quiet orchestra stretches out a long ways past the lines of individual environments.

The complex snare of life isn't without its difficulties, and the quiet orchestra is helpless against interruptions brought about by human exercises.

Deforestation, environment obliteration, contamination, and environmental change bring dissonant notes into the orchestra, compromising the sensitive equilibrium that has advanced over centuries. The results of these interruptions reverberation through environments, affecting biodiversity, and compromising the strength of the normal world.

Understanding the quiet orchestra requires an investigation of the job of mankind inside this many-sided sythesis. As stewards of the Earth, people have the ability to either improve the amicable equilibrium or disturb the sensitive arrangement of nature. Our decisions, from land use and asset extraction to preservation endeavors and supportable practices, impact the general tune of the ensemble. Perceiving our obligation in this aggregate undertaking is vital for the safeguarding of the quiet orchestra.

The idea of collecting nature's quiet orchestra arises as a figurative excursion inside the more extensive investigation of the components adding to the ensemble. It includes dependable commitment with the normal world, recognizing the characteristic worth of biodiversity, and encouraging a feeling of stewardship that rises above ages. Collecting, in this unique circumstance, is a source of inspiration - a call to receive the rewards of nature while guaranteeing the protection of the sensitive equilibrium that supports life.

Native people group, with their profound association with the land and customary information, become central members in the ensemble's sythesis. Their amicable conjunction with nature, went down through ages, offers significant experiences into reasonable practices and the protection of biodiversity. The insight of native societies turns into a tune inside the orchestra, helping us to remember the significance of living as one with the Earth.

Innovative headways, with their capability to both guide and disturb the ensemble, acquaint a unique component with the story. From observing environments and understanding biodiversity to moderating the effects of human exercises, innovation can be a useful asset in the safeguarding of the quiet ensemble. Nonetheless, it is critical to work out some kind of harmony, guaranteeing that mechanical advancement lines up with the standards of biological manageability.

The orchestra broadens its impact into the domains of craftsmanship, culture, and otherworldliness, stressing the significant effect of nature on the human mind. Craftsmen draw motivation from the excellence of scenes, artists track down comfort in the serenity of nature, and profound customs commend the interconnectedness of every living thing. The quiet orchestra turns into a dream for innovative articulation, inciting reflection on the inherent worth of the normal world.

All in all, making way for the investigation of the components adding to Nature's Quiet Ensemble requires an all encompassing comprehension of the complicated dance of life on The planet. Biodiversity, biological systems, life cycles, abiotic factors, hunter prey connections, movement designs, and the job of mankind all merge to make an agreeable piece that rises above the perceptible. The quiet ensemble welcomes us to tune in, to comprehend, and to become dynamic members in the protection of the sensitive equilibrium that supports life on this unprecedented planet. As we set out on this investigation, we are called to see the value in the subtleties of the ensemble, perceive our job inside it, and focus on an aggregate work to guarantee its progression for a long time into the future.

In the tremendous and complex embroidered artwork of the regular world, Nature's Quiet Orchestra unfurls, winding around together the different components that add to the agreeable equilibrium of life on The planet. This orchestra, albeit quiet to the human ear, resounds through the interconnected elements of biological systems, the multifaceted connections among species, and the interminable patterns of life and passing. To dig into the investigation of the different components adding to this orchestra is to leave on an excursion through the mind boggling trap of biodiversity, the unique transaction of environments, and the significant impact of human activities on the sythesis of this quiet however significant show-stopper.

At the core of Nature's Quiet Ensemble lies biodiversity, the extraordinary assortment of life shapes that occupy our planet. Biodiversity envelops the whole range of living creatures, from tiny microbes to transcending trees and from the littlest bugs to glorious vertebrates. Every species inside this immense organic symphony assumes an exceptional part, contributing its unmistakable song to the general organization. The lavishness of biodiversity isn't just a scene; it is the actual quintessence of the ensemble, forming environments, impacting biological cycles, and supporting life.

Environments act as the fantastic stages whereupon Nature's Quiet Ensemble is performed. These mind boggling and dynamic networks of living creatures interface with their actual climate, making different natural surroundings that help a horde of living things. From rainforests overflowing with biodiversity to the obvious excellence of deserts, every biological system has its own arrangement of entertainers, each having their impact in the mind boggling dance of the ensemble. Environments are not segregated elements; rather, they are interconnected, framing an organization that traverses the globe, working with the trading of energy, supplements, and life.

The patterns of life and passing inside biological systems structure essential developments inside the quiet orchestra. Birth, development, propagation, and rot comprise the ceaseless beat that supports the equilibrium of nature. Each life form, from the littlest microorganism to the biggest hunter, assumes a part in these cycles.

Decomposers, frequently neglected in the fabulous story of nature, are quiet guides, separating natural matter and reusing supplements once again into the biological system. The agreeable progression of life and passing guarantees the recharging and strength of biological systems.

Abiotic factors, the non-living parts of environments, give the background against which the orchestra unfurls. Soil, water, daylight, and environment are fundamental components that impact the circulation and conduct of species. The accessibility of these abiotic factors decides the design of biological systems and shapes the tunes of the ensemble. Changes in environment, whether regular or anthropogenic, can modify the beat and elements of the ensemble, influencing the existence cycles, ways of behaving, and circulation of species.

Hunter prey connections present a sensational and fundamental dynamic to Nature's Quiet Orchestra. Hunters and prey participate in a never-ending dance of life and demise, molding the design and working of biological systems. Hunters assume a vital part in directing prey populaces, forestalling overgrazing or overconsumption of assets. Prey species, thusly, foster variations and techniques to avoid predation, adding to the unpredictable and fragile equilibrium inside environments. The nonattendance or lopsidedness of these connections can prompt biological interruptions, influencing the general strength of the ensemble.

Relocation designs structure one more mind boggling development inside the quiet orchestra, interfacing biological systems across immense distances. Birds, vertebrates, and even bugs set out on awe-inspiring excursions, adding to the trading of hereditary material, working with fertilization, and impacting the biodiversity of numerous areas. Relocation highlights the worldwide interconnectedness of nature, exhibiting that the quiet ensemble reaches out a long ways past the boundaries of individual environments. It is a demonstration of the ease and network of life on The planet.

The perplexing trap of life isn't resistant to the difficulties presented by human exercises. Deforestation, environment obliteration, contamination, and environmental change bring grating notes into Nature's Quiet Ensemble, compromising the sensitive equilibrium that has advanced north of millions of years. The outcomes of these interruptions reverberation through biological systems, affecting biodiversity, and compromising the flexibility of the normal world. Human activities, both on the whole and independently, have the ability to either upgrade the agreeable equilibrium or upset the fragile arrangement of the quiet ensemble.

Mankind's part in the ensemble turns into a point of convergence in understanding and protecting Nature's Quiet Orchestra. As stewards of the Earth, people have the ability to impact the course and rhythm of the orchestra. Decisions connected with land use, asset extraction, protection endeavors, and reasonable practices can either fit with the regular rhythms or present cacophony. Perceiving this obligation is principal to guaranteeing the safeguarding of the fragile equilibrium that portrays the quiet ensemble.

The idea of reaping nature's quiet ensemble arises as a figurative excursion inside the more extensive investigation of the components adding to the orchestra. Reaping, in this unique situation, is certainly not a simple extraction of assets for human addition; rather, it is a figurative and equal cooperation with nature. It includes recognizing the inherent worth of biodiversity, understanding the natural administrations that biological systems give, and cultivating a feeling of stewardship that rises above ages. It is a source of inspiration - a call to receive the rewards of nature mindfully, with a consciousness of the fragile equilibrium that supports life.

Native people group, with their profound association with the land and customary information, become vital participants in the ensemble's organization. Their amicable concurrence with nature, went down through ages, offers significant experiences into supportable practices and the protection of biodiversity. Native insight turns into a song inside the orchestra, helping us to remember the significance of living as one with the Earth and regarding the mind boggling equilibrium of nature.

Innovative progressions, with their capability to both guide and disturb the ensemble, acquaint a unique component with the story. From observing biological systems and understanding biodiversity to moderating the effects of human exercises, innovation can be an integral asset in the protection of Nature's Quiet Ensemble. In any case, it is urgent to figure out some kind of harmony, guaranteeing that mechanical advancement lines up with the standards of biological manageability. The mindful utilization of innovation can add to how we might interpret environments and help in the preservation endeavors that are fundamental for saving the quiet ensemble.

The ensemble expands its impact into the domains of craftsmanship, culture, and otherworldliness, underscoring the significant effect of nature on the human mind. Craftsmen draw motivation from the excellence of scenes, writers track down comfort in the serenity of nature, and otherworldly customs praise the interconnectedness of every living thing. The quiet orchestra turns into a dream for innovative articulation, provoking reflection on the inborn worth of the normal world and the significant associations that tight spot all life.

All in all, investigating the components adding to Nature's Quiet Ensemble is an excursion into the actual texture of life on The planet. Biodiversity, biological systems, life cycles, abiotic factors, hunter prey connections, movement designs, and the job of humankind all meet to make an agreeable piece that rises above the discernible. The quiet ensemble welcomes us to tune in, to comprehend, and to become dynamic members in the safeguarding of the sensitive equilibrium that supports life on this remarkable planet. As we leave on this investigation, we are called to see the value in the subtleties of the orchestra, perceive our job inside it, and focus on an aggregate work to guarantee its coherence for a long time into the future.

Chapter 2

The Rhythm of Seasons

In the tremendous embroidery of presence, the beat of seasons winds around an immortal song, a steadily changing ensemble that coordinates the dance of life on The planet. Nature, with its endless imagination, spreads out an exhibition that unfurls in cycles, an entrancing continuum that shapes the actual embodiment of our reality.

As winter's frigid fingers grasp the land in a chilly hug, a quieted tranquility settles upon the earth. The world appears to pause its breathing, trapped in the frigid grasp of the time. Trees stand exposed, their branches arriving at like skeletal fingers toward a cold and far off sun. The scene, once dynamic with the tints of pre-winter, presently lies lethargic, calmly anticipating the commitment of recharging.

However, underneath the frozen surface, life continues in a calm sleep. Seeds lie settled in the dirt, supported by the world's defensive hug. Creatures, adjusted to the brutal circumstances, move with conscious reason through the snow-shrouded scenes. It is a time of endurance, where perseverance and flexibility become the money of life.

As winter respects the delicate touch of spring, the world stirs from its frigid sleep. The air is imbued with the lovely fragrance of blooms, and the scene changes into a mob of varieties. Nature, similar to a talented painter, strokes the material of the earth with dynamic tints, as though declaring the appearance of a fresh start.

The ensemble of life crescendos as verdure answer the evolving rhythms. Trees spread out fragile leaves, blossoms sprout in a mob of varieties, and the air is buzzing with the murmur of bugs and the song of birdsong. Life blasts forward in a festival of recharging, a demonstration of the unyielding soul of the regular world.

With the coming of summer, the sun rises to its pinnacle, projecting a warm and big-hearted shine upon the earth. The days stretch drowsily, welcoming life to luxuriate in the overflow of daylight. The world turns into an energetic embroidery of green, as the verdure comes to towards the sky, inebriated by the energy of the sun.

Summer is a time of overflow, where the world's abundance is revealed so anyone might be able to see. Fields of brilliant grain influence in the breeze, a demonstration of the farming rhythms that have supported developments for centuries. Creatures wander unreservedly, touching on the rich fields, and the air is loaded up with the energetic murmur of bugs.

However, even amidst overflow, there is a fundamental consciousness of fleetingness. The sun, however kind, starts its sluggish drop towards the skyline, flagging the unavoidable shift towards the following period of the occasional ensemble. As summer fades, a feeling of calm reflection plummets upon the land, as though nature itself is pausing for a minute to stop and relax.

Harvest time shows up with a twist of varieties, as though nature is putting on a last, stunning showcase before the inescapable drop into winter's hug. The air is fresh with the fragrance of fallen leaves, and the scene is painted in tones of red, orange, and gold. Trees, when lavish with plant life, shed their foliage in a smooth acquiescence to the evolving season.

Fall is a time of change, an extension between the glow of summer and the chill of winter. The world gets ready for the approaching hibernation, as creatures accumulate arrangements and the last remnants of life retreat into the earth. There is a tangible feeling of conclusion, an acknowledgment that the pattern of life is approaching its fulfillment.

As winter returns, the cycle starts once again. The earth, by and by covered in snow, enters a time of lethargy. The orchestra of life, however muffled, go on underneath the frozen surface. Seeds stand by without complaining for their second to grow, and creatures explore the difficulties of the virus season with emotionless assurance.

The musicality of seasons isn't simply a pattern of birth, development, and lethargy; it is a representation for the rhythmic movement of life itself. It reflects the human experience, with its times of euphoria and distress, development and stagnation. Each season holds an illustration, an update that change is unavoidable and that, in each consummation, there is the seed of a fresh start.

In the mood of seasons, there is a significant interconnectedness that ties generally living things. The sensitive equilibrium of nature is a demonstration of the mind boggling trap of connections that supports life on The planet. Plants depend on creatures for fertilization, and creatures rely upon plants for food. The changing seasons organize an amicable dance, where every member assumes an essential part in the terrific embroidery of life.

However, the musicality of seasons is certainly not a static creation; it is a dynamic and consistently developing orchestra. Human exercises, with their significant effect on the climate, have brought cacophony into the normal song. Environmental change, deforestation, and contamination disturb the fragile equilibrium that has supported life for centuries, undermining the actual texture of the occasional mood.

As we demonstrate the veracity of the outcomes of our activities, there is a squeezing need to rediscover our association with the normal world. The musicality of seasons fills in as a strong update that we are not isolated from nature but rather a necessary piece of it. Our prosperity is unpredictably connected to the strength of the planet, and our activities echo through the trap of life, influencing each living being.

Notwithstanding ecological difficulties, there is a dire source of inspiration, an aggregate liability to shield the beat of seasons for people in the future. Protection endeavors, maintainable practices, and a careful way to deal with utilization are fundamental stages towards reestablishing the fragile equilibrium that supports life on The planet.

The beat of seasons, with its ageless rhythm, welcomes us to consider the recurrent idea of presence. It instructs us that, amidst life's variances, there is a more profound request that ties everything together. Similarly as the seasons consistently progress starting with one then onto the next, so too does life unfurl in a nonstop pattern of progress and recharging.

In the thought of nature's rhythms, there is a chance for significant understanding and shrewdness. The changing seasons become a mirror, mirroring the fleetingness of all things and the innate excellence of the current second. Each season, with its remarkable characteristics, welcomes us to embrace the full range of our human experience.

As we explore the flows of life, the mood of seasons turns into a directing power, offering comfort in the midst of difficulty and motivation in snapshots of bliss. It is an update that, regardless of how testing the colder time of year might be, spring will definitely follow, carrying with it the commitment of fresh starts. Moreover, in the level of summer's overflow, there is an unobtrusive murmur of harvest time, a delicate sign of the transient idea, everything being equal.

The beat of seasons rises above geological limits, social contrasts, and individual viewpoints. A general language addresses the interconnectedness of all life. Whether underneath Aurora Borealis or under the Southern Cross, whether in the clamoring city or the peaceful wild, the musicality of seasons ties us together in a common excursion through the embroidery of presence.

In the calm examination of a snow-shrouded scene or the lively explosion of cherry blooms, we settle on something worth agreeing on that rises above the divisions that frequently isolated us. The cadence of seasons welcomes us to praise our variety while perceiving our common humankind. It is an update that, notwithstanding our disparities, we are travelers on a similar spaceship Earth, exploring the tremendous enormous ocean together.

In the terrific embroidery of presence, the musicality of seasons is a demonstration of the flexibility and excellence of life. It is an account of resurrection and restoration, of cycles that rise above the limits of time. As we adjust ourselves to the inconspicuous songs of nature, we are welcome to hit the dance floor with the mood of seasons, to embrace the consistently evolving, always recharging stream of life.

In the dance of life, there is a challenge to develop a profound feeling of love and appreciation for the planet that supports us. The mood of seasons is a gift, a well-spring of motivation that helps us to remember our interconnectedness with every living thing. It is a call to esteem and safeguard the fragile equilibrium that permits life to prosper on this wondrous blue planet.

As we leave on the excursion of each season, let us proceed with caution upon the earth, aware of the effect of our strides. Allow us to develop a feeling of stewardship, perceiving that we are endowed with the prosperity of the planet for people in the future. In the cadence of seasons, we track down a significant greeting to live as one with the normal world, to respect the sacredness of life in the entirety of its structures.

In the tranquil snapshots of reflection, as the snow falls tenderly or the leaves stir in the harvest time breeze, let us pay attention to the murmurs of nature. Allow us to regard the insight implanted in the cadence of seasons, an insight that rises above the restrictions of language and culture. An insight addresses the heart, welcoming us to proceed with caution, love profoundly, and live as one with the consistently evolving, steadily restoring dance of life.

2.1 Delve into the cyclical patterns of seasons and their impact on the natural world.

The repetitive examples of seasons weave a mind boggling embroidery of progress across the material of the normal world, coordinating an interminable dance that has molded the course of life on Earth for ages. These occasional rhythms, represented by the slant of the planet's hub and its circle around the sun, manifest as winter, spring, summer, and harvest time, each with its special person and effect on the climate.

Winter, the time of lethargy and quietness, covers the earth in a peaceful quiet. The air crisps with cold, and the scene goes through a change as snow covers the ground. Trees stand exposed, their branches scratched against the colder time of year sky like sensitive lacework. It is a period of retreat, a period when the normal world appears to draw internal, saving energy for the pattern of recharging that lies ahead.

In this season, the effect on the regular world is significant. Many plants, especially deciduous trees, enter a condition of lethargy, shedding leaves and coordinating their assets internal. Creatures adjust to the cool, a few resting in tunnels or homes, while others foster thick winter coats for protection. The frozen surfaces of lakes and streams limit oceanic action, making a brief respite in the energetic biological systems that flourish underneath the water's surface.

However, even in the appearing torpidity of winter, life continues. Underneath the snow-made progress, seeds lie lethargic, trusting that the glow of spring will stir them from their sleep. Creatures, however less noticeable, proceed with their day to day schedules, depending on transformations and systems to explore the difficulties of the virus season. Winter, with its cold breath, is a vital piece of the occasional cycle, making way for the changes that follow.

As winter slowly respects the delicate hug of spring, the regular world goes through a transformation. The air warms, and the main indications of something going on under the surface arise as buds spread out on branches and blossoms burst forward from the defrosting ground. Spring is a time of resurrection, a festival of restoration that brings an explosion of variety and imperativeness to the scene.

The effect of spring on the regular world is maybe most clear in the peculiarity of blooming plants. Trees, bushes, and wildflowers sprout in a mob of varieties, their petals drawing in pollinators in a dance of harmonious connections. Honey bees, butterflies, and different pollinators assume a urgent part in this season, working with the generation of plants and adding to the variety of environments.

Spring additionally denotes the arrival of transient birds, as they venture immense distances to favorable places. The air is loaded up with the resonant melodies of birds, adding a melodic quality to the ensemble of the time.

Creatures rise up out of winter covers, and the energy of life beats through the scene as the pattern of development and recovery becomes the overwhelming focus.

With the coming of summer, the regular world arrives at a zenith of overflow and essentialness. The sun rises to its pinnacle, projecting a warm sparkle over the earth. The effect of summer on environments is significant, as the expanded daylight fills photosynthesis, the cycle by which plants convert daylight into energy. This flood in energy overflows through the well established pecking order, supporting the development of vegetation and supporting assorted networks of herbivores and carnivores.

In summer, environments overflow with life. Timberlands are rich with vegetation, and knolls burst forward with a kaleidoscope of wildflowers. Oceanic environments, warmed by the sun, become energetic centers of movement as fish, creatures of land and water, and bugs flourish in the wealth of supplements. The long days and warm evenings give sufficient chances to creatures to scrounge, chase, and recreate, adding to the never-ending pattern of life.

The effect of summer is likewise apparent in the farming scenes developed by people. Fields of yields, from brilliant wheat to verdant corn, arrive at their top during this season. Ranchers bridle the sun's energy to develop plentiful harvests, and the abundance of summer supports networks with a rich embroidery of natural products, vegetables, and grains.

However, amidst summer's overflow, there is a propensity of temporariness. The sun, however big-hearted, starts its slow drop towards the skyline, flagging the coming progress to the following period of the occasional cycle. As the days gradually abbreviate, there is an unpretentious change in the air, an update that the wheel of time keeps on turning.

Fall, with its fresh air and lively foliage, denotes a time of progress and reflection. The effect of fall is noticeable in the changing shades of deciduous trees, as chlorophyll separates, uncovering the reds, oranges, and yellows of colors that were veiled during the developing season. The scene changes into a visual exhibition, a demonstration of the repeating idea of life.

In harvest time, environments plan for the approaching winter. Trees, once decorated with leaves, shed their foliage as a methodology to preserve energy and water.

Creatures take part in furious action, gathering food and getting ready sanctuaries for the cool a long time ahead. Transient birds, having finished their reproducing season, set out on excursions to hotter environments, abandoning a calmer scene.

The effect of pre-winter stretches out past the visual wonder of falling leaves. It is a time of collect, when people and natural life the same assemble the mid year's rewards for so much hard work.

Ranchers get the last yields of harvests, and animals rummage for nuts, seeds, and different assets to support them through the colder time of year. Fall is a time of over-flow, yet it likewise conveys a demeanor of goodbye, a strong sign of the brevity innate in the pattern of seasons.

As fall gives method for wintering, the normal world by and by enters a time of lethargy. The effect of winter is a continuation of the recurrent mood, an important stage that permits biological systems to rest and revive. Snow covers the ground, protecting it from the most extreme temperatures, and the frozen surfaces of waterways make a transitory delay in the sea-going biological systems.

Plants and creatures adjust to the difficulties of winter in different ways. A few animal varieties, similar to evergreen trees, hold their leaves, keeping a similarity to plant life against the colder time of year background. Others, similar to well evolved creatures and birds, have created particular variations, for example, thicker fur or plumes to endure the virus. The hibernation of specific creatures is an exceptional methodology to save energy during the time of shortage.

In the profundities of winter, the effect on the normal world might appear to be curbed, yet life continues underneath the frozen surface. Seeds stand by without complaining in the dirt, prepared to sprout when the glow of spring shows up. Micro-organisms in the dirt proceed with their fundamental work, breaking down natural matter and reusing supplements. Winter, however a time of torpidity, is a fundamental piece of the cycle that readies the stage for the restoration of life.

The repetitive examples of seasons are not just a demonstration of the strength of the normal world yet additionally a wellspring of motivation for human societies across time and geology. The changing seasons have been woven into the texture of legends, fables, and customs, mirroring a profound comprehension of the inter-connectedness among people and the climate.

In many societies, the seasons are related with divinities or spirits that oversee the patterns of nature. Customs and festivities mark the advances between seasons, recognizing the meaning of each stage in the great embroidered artwork of life. The effect of occasional changes isn't simply noticed however effectively took part in, encouraging a feeling of concordance and correspondence between human networks and the normal world.

The horticultural acts of antiquated developments were frequently intently attached to the patterns of seasons. Planting and reaping were coordinated to line up with the ideal states of each season, and the progress of yields was complicatedly connected to a comprehension of the normal rhythms. This close information on the seasons was gone down through ages, framing the premise of practical farming customs.

In current times, the effect of occasional changes stretches out past the domains of farming to impact different parts of human existence. Occasional emotional problem (Miserable), a sort of despondency that happens at explicit seasons, is one illustration of what the changing seasons can mean for psychological wellness. The diminished openness to daylight throughout the cold weather months is remembered to add to the improvement of Miserable, featuring the mind boggling exchange between natural elements and human prosperity.

Besides, the repeating examples of seasons assume a vital part in forming biological systems and biodiversity. The planning of occasional occasions, like blossoming, movement, and propagation, is finely tuned to ecological prompts. Any disturbance to this synchrony, whether because of environmental change or other anthropogenic elements, can have flowing impacts on the fragile equilibrium of biological systems.

Environmental change, driven by human exercises like the consuming of petroleum derivatives and deforestation, represents a critical danger to the conventional examples of seasons. Increasing worldwide temperatures, changed precipitation examples, and more incessant outrageous climate occasions can disturb the finely tuned rhythms that biological systems have developed to rely on. The effect of these progressions resounds through the trap of life, influencing everything from the planning of plant blooming to the relocation examples of birds.

Even with these difficulties, there is a developing acknowledgment of the requirement for protection and supportable practices to moderate the effect of environmental change on the occasional cycles. Endeavors to safeguard regular environments, decrease ozone harming substance outflows, and advance economical asset the board are pivotal strides towards saving the fragile equilibrium that supports life on The planet.

Diving into the recurrent examples of seasons welcomes us to mull over the significant interconnectedness of all life. The effect of occasional changes rises above individual species, biological systems, and geographic limits. A general beat ties generally living things in a common excursion through the embroidery of presence.

As we explore the consistently changing scene of our reality, there is a squeezing need for a recharged enthusiasm for the normal rhythms that support life. The effect of human exercises on the climate highlights the desperation of embracing maintainable practices and encouraging a feeling of stewardship for the planet. The repetitive examples of seasons, with their immortal rhythm, allure us to adjust our activities to the amicable dance of the normal world.

In the calm consideration of a snow-shrouded scene or the dynamic eruption of spring blooms, we find a mirror mirroring the repeating idea of our own lives.

The effect of occasional changes turns into a representation for the recurring pattern of human encounters, the certainty of progress, and the ceaseless chance for restoration. Each season, with its interesting characteristics, turns into an instructor, welcoming us to embrace the full range of our reality.

In the fabulous orchestra of life, the recurrent examples of seasons are a tune that resounds across existence. A song rises above language, culture, and individual points of view. Whether underneath Aurora Borealis or under the Southern Cross, whether in the clamoring city or the tranquil wild, the effect of seasons joins us in a common excursion through the huge vast embroidery.

In the investigation of occasional cycles, there is a challenge to develop a profound feeling of love for the planet that supports us. The repeating examples of seasons are a gift, a wellspring of motivation that helps us to remember our interconnectedness with every single living thing. They are a call to love and safeguard the sensitive equilibrium that permits life to prosper on this wondrous blue planet.

As we dive into the recurrent examples of seasons, let us proceed with caution upon the earth, aware of the effect of our strides. Allow us to develop a feeling of stunningness and marvel for the perplexing trap of life that encompasses us. In the hug of nature's rhythms, we find an immortal insight that rises above the limits of our singular viewpoints.

The recurrent examples of seasons entice us to live as one with the regular world, to respect the sacredness of life in the entirety of its structures. As we adjust ourselves to the unpretentious tunes of nature, we are welcome to hit the dance floor with the mood of seasons, to embrace the consistently evolving, always restoring stream of life. In the dance of seasons, we track down a significant greeting to reside with appreciation, lowliness, and a profound appreciation for the phenomenal endowment of presence on this eminent planet we call home.

2.2 Highlight the role of seasonal changes in shaping the behavior of flora and fauna.

Occasional changes, the cadenced beat of nature, assume a urgent part in shaping the way of behaving of verdure. This mind boggling dance, arranged by the slant of the World's hub and its circle around the sun, organizes an orchestra of reactions from the different occupants of the normal world. From the tiny to the glorious, each organic entity is receptive to the repetitive examples of the seasons, and these progressions significantly impact their way of behaving, physiology, and life cycles.

Greenery, the quiet designers of scenes, are maybe the most apparently receptive to occasional movements. As winter plummets and temperatures decrease, deciduous trees, like maples and oaks, answer by shedding their leaves.

This versatile procedure permits them to preserve water and energy during the colder months when daylight is less plentiful. The effect on the scene is striking, as trees change from lively shelters of green to unmistakable outlines against the colder time of year sky.

Alternately, evergreen trees, like pines and tidies, hold their needles consistently. This variation empowers them to proceed with photosynthesis, the cycle by which they convert daylight into energy, even in the cold weather months. The unobtrusive stirring of evergreen branches in the colder time of year breeze is a demonstration of their strength, as they continue giving a dash of plant life in the midst of the colder time of year's lethargy.

With the appearance of spring, greenery go through a restoration, answering the rising sunlight and warming temperatures. Buds grow and spread out into leaves, and torpid seeds stir from their colder time of year sleep. The effect on the scene is an eruption of variety and imperativeness, as wildflowers cover the ground, and the once-exposed parts of trees are decorated with blooms.

The job of occasional changes stretches out past the visual scene of blooming plants. In the domain of regenerative techniques, many plants depend on occasional signs to synchronize their endeavors. Spring, with its ideal circumstances, is an inclined toward time for blooming and fertilization. Honey bees, butterflies, and different pollinators become dynamic, attracted to the nectar and dust created by blossoms. This mutualistic relationship is a demonstration of the multifaceted trap of reliance woven by the seasons.

The effect of occasional changes on vegetation reaches out to the planning of seed creation. As summer unfurls and the days extend, plants channel their energy into creating seeds. The timing is vital, guaranteeing that seeds are prepared for dispersal before the appearance of winter. A few plants, similar to sunflowers, show a note-worthy heliotropic conduct, following the sun's development across the sky to boost their openness and seed creation.

Pre-winter, a time of progress, proclaims one more change in the way of behaving of verdure. Deciduous trees, having filled their need in the developing season, go through senescence. The effect on leaves is a stunning exhibit of varieties as chloro-phyll separates, uncovering the colors that had been covered. The falling leaves cover the ground, shaping a defensive layer that supports the dirt and sets it up for the approaching winter.

While greenery answer noticeably to occasional changes, fauna, the different cluster of creature life, display a scope of ways of behaving that are unpredictably connected to the recurrent rhythms of the climate. Movement is one of the most surprising and proven and factual reactions to occasional changes, saw in various species across the globe.

Birds, specifically, are prestigious for their transitory excursions. As winter draws near, many bird species set out on amazing movements to hotter environments where food and it are more bountiful to settle open doors. The effect of movement isn't simply an issue of endurance yet in addition a dynamite accomplishment of persever-ance and route. From the Cold tern, which goes from one post to another, to the ruler butterfly, which traverses mainlands, movement is an amazing variation to the difficulties introduced by evolving seasons.

The reproducing ways of behaving of fauna are likewise complicatedly attached to occasional prompts. Spring, with its warming temperatures and expanded light, sets off a flood in conceptive movement. Creatures of land and water, like frogs, take part in chorales of calls to draw in mates to rearing locales. Bugs, from fireflies to cicadas, arise in enormous numbers for romance ceremonies. The effect on biological systems is a whirlwind of movement as creatures commit energy to generation, guaranteeing the continuation of their species.

The planning of proliferation is frequently synchronized with the accessibility of assets. For well evolved creatures in calm environments, the introduction of posterity is frequently coordinated to harmonize with the wealth of food in spring or late-spring. This guarantees that youthful creatures approach a rich food supply during their underlying progressive phases. The effect on populaces is a flood in births, making a companion of youthful people ready to confront the difficulties of the world.

Hibernation is one more noteworthy conduct showed by specific fauna in light of occasional changes. As winter approaches and food turns out to be scant, a few warm blooded creatures, like bears and groundhogs, enter a condition of lethargy. The effect of hibernation is a decrease in metabolic action, permitting these creatures to ration energy and make due through the cold weather months when assets are restricted. This transformation features the noteworthy adaptability of fauna in changing their way of behaving to the difficulties presented via occasional variances.

The amphibian domain, as well, encounters the effect of occasional changes on fauna conduct. Many fish species, for instance, take part in producing relocations. As temperatures climb in the spring, fish move upstream to bring forth in freshwater natural surroundings. The effect on freshwater biological systems is significant, as the inundation of supplements from generating occasions adds to the imperativeness of these environments.

In marine conditions, the way of behaving of marine vertebrates is firmly connected to the accessibility of food. Whales, for example, embrace broad relocations looking for prey. The effect of these relocations isn't just an issue of endurance for the whales yet in addition assumes a pivotal part in marine biological systems by reallocating supplements and impacting the construction of food networks.

The effect of occasional changes on fauna conduct isn't restricted to earthbound and sea-going conditions yet stretches out to the heap animals occupying assorted environments, from deserts to rainforests. Every species has developed explicit variations to adapt to the difficulties presented by the evolving seasons, making a mosaic of ways of behaving that add to the general strength and biodiversity of the regular world.

Besides, the interconnectedness of vegetation in occasional ways of behaving is obvious in the mind boggling snare of connections that characterize environments. For instance, the fertilization ways of behaving of honey bees and butterflies are essential for the propagation of blooming plants. The effect of this mutualistic relationship resonates through the pecking order, as it guarantees the development of foods grown from the ground that act as food for various creatures.

The occasional way of behaving of fauna isn't just formed by the ecological signs of temperature and light yet additionally by the mind boggling communications between species. Hunter prey connections, rivalry for assets, and advantageous associations all add to the powerful embroidered artwork of ways of behaving saw in the normal world.

As environmental change speeds up, adjusting the customary examples of seasons, there is developing worry about the effect on the way of behaving of vegetation. Changes in temperature, precipitation, and the planning of seasons can disturb the finely tuned connections among species and make difficulties for the endurance of specific populaces.

For example, changes in the planning of blooming and fertilization can prompt a befuddle among plants and their pollinators, risking the conceptive progress of both. The effect of these disturbances reaches out to the creatures that rely upon foods grown from the ground for food. Changes in movement designs, reproducing times, and hibernation ways of behaving are seen across different species, featuring the weakness of biological systems to environment prompted modifications in occasional signals.

Preservation endeavors, accordingly, progressively accentuate the need to safeguard and reestablish natural surroundings, decrease anthropogenic effects on the climate, and moderate the impacts of environmental change. Safeguarding the regular rhythms of occasional changes isn't just pivotal for the endurance of individual species yet additionally for keeping up with the flexibility and usefulness of biological systems all in all.

All in all, the effect of occasional changes on the way of behaving of greenery is a demonstration of the complexities of life on The planet. The recurrent examples of seasons act as a directing power, forming the physiological reactions, regenerative techniques, and movement ways of behaving of the different occupants of the regular world. The fragile dance between natural signs and versatile reactions makes an orchestra of life that supports the magnificence and biodiversity of our planet.

As stewards of the Earth, it is our obligation to comprehend and value the job of occasional changes in shaping the way of behaving of widely varied vegetation. Protection endeavors, feasible practices, and a profound regard for the interconnected trap of life are fundamental to guaranteeing that the effect of occasional changes keeps on winding around its immortal story through the scenes, seas, and skies of our wondrous planet.

2.3 Discuss the importance of understanding and respecting these natural rhythms.

Understanding and regarding the normal rhythms implanted in the patterns of the Earth is central for both the prosperity of the planet and the thriving of all life that calls it home. These complex examples, appeared in the changing seasons and the ways of behaving of widely varied vegetation, are not simple peculiarities to be noticed; they structure the actual texture of the interconnected trap of life. Digging into the significance of fathoming and respecting these normal rhythms uncovers a significant acknowledgment of our position in the great embroidery of presence.

At the center of this significance lies the acknowledgment that the Earth isn't simply a uninvolved stage for human exercises yet a living, unique element with its own rhythms and cycles. The evolving seasons, driven by the slant of the World's pivot and its circle around the sun, oversee the rhythmic movement of life. Understanding these normal rhythms is to recognize that our reality is personally interlaced with the heartbeat of the planet, and our activities have broad outcomes on the fragile equilibrium that supports life.

Regarding these regular rhythms is a call to adjust our exercises to the innate insight of the Earth. The effect of human activities, from modern exercises to deforestation, has disturbed these rhythms, prompting ecological debasement and the deficiency of biodiversity. By getting it and regarding the normal cycles, we can develop an agreeable relationship with the planet, one that recognizes our job as stewards instead of exploiters of the World's assets.

One of the essential motivations to comprehend and regard regular rhythms is the protection of biodiversity. The perplexing dance of verdure, synchronized with the evolving seasons, adds to the lavishness and variety of biological systems. Every species assumes a novel part in keeping up with the wellbeing and usefulness of the biological system, from pollinators guaranteeing the generation of plants to hunters directing prey populaces. Disturbing these normal rhythms can prompt awkward nature that fountain through the pecking order, compromising the solidness of whole biological systems.

Besides, biodiversity isn't just a proportion of the quantity of species yet additionally mirrors the hereditary variety inside populaces. The flexibility of species to changing natural circumstances depends on hereditary variety.

By regarding the normal rhythms that oversee the way of behaving and life patterns of organic entities, we add to the safeguarding of hereditary variety, guaranteeing that species can adjust and develop because of natural changes.

Understanding and regarding normal rhythms are likewise indispensable for the arrangement of environment administrations. Environments, formed by the repeating examples of seasons and the cooperations between species, offer fundamental types of assistance that help human prosperity. These administrations incorporate clean air and water, fertilization of yields, guideline of environment, and the arrangement of food and medication. Upsetting the normal rhythms of biological systems endangers the conveyance of these administrations, influencing human social orders that depend on them for endurance and success.

Horticulture, a basic mainstay of human development, is complicatedly attached to the regular rhythms of the Earth. Conventional cultivating rehearses have developed to line up with the evolving seasons, deciding the planning of planting, gathering, and neglected periods. Understanding and regarding these regular rhythms in farming lead to manageable practices that upgrade efficiency while limiting natural effect. Present day modern agribusiness, frequently separated from the repeating examples of seasons, has prompted issues like soil corruption, water exhaustion, and loss of biodiversity.

Besides, the effect of environmental change highlights the direness of understanding and regarding normal rhythms. Human exercises, especially the consuming of petroleum products and deforestation, have adjusted the structure of the air, prompting a dangerous atmospheric devation and changes in precipitation designs. These progressions disturb the customary examples of seasons, prompting more continuous and extreme climate occasions, changes in developing seasons, and modified relocation designs for both earthly and marine species.

Regarding normal rhythms turns into a basic part of environmental change relief and variation. Feasible practices that decrease ozone depleting substance emanations, save timberlands, and advance the reclamation of biological systems add to the strength of the planet even with environment challenges. Understanding the repetitive examples of seasons considers better expectations of environment related influences, empowering networks to get ready and adjust to changes in their surroundings.

Past the substantial advantages for biological systems and environment, understanding and regarding regular rhythms hold significant ramifications for human prosperity. The effect of nature on human wellbeing and mental prosperity is indisputable. Openness to regular habitats, with their occasional varieties, has been connected to diminished pressure, worked on mental capability, and improved by and large psychological wellness. Regarding normal rhythms is, in this way, an acknowledgment of the equal connection among people and the climate, recognizing that our wellbeing is unpredictably associated with the strength of the planet.

Social and otherworldly aspects further intensify the significance of understanding and regarding normal rhythms. All through mankind's set of experiences, social orders have woven occasional cycles into their folklores, customs, and ceremonies. The effect of seasons on social practices is apparent in festivals, functions, and celebrations that mark the advances among winter and spring, summer and fall. Regarding regular rhythms is an approach to respecting the insight implanted in these social works on, cultivating a more profound association among mankind and the Earth.

Native societies, specifically, have kept up with significant associations with the regular world, directed by a profound comprehension of the repeating examples of seasons. The effect of these societies on the protection of biodiversity and practical asset the executives is critical. Native information, went down through ages, holds significant experiences into living as one with the Earth. Regarding regular rhythms requires recognizing the insight implanted in native practices and teaming up with these networks to advance preservation and maintainability.

In the domain of training, understanding and regarding normal rhythms give an establishment to environmental education. As people in the future explore an undeniably perplexing and interconnected world, a consciousness of the recurrent examples of seasons cultivates a feeling of obligation and stewardship. Ecological training that integrates the effect of human exercises on normal rhythms enables people to settle on informed decisions that add to a feasible and regenerative future.

Mechanical progressions, while offering answers for some difficulties, likewise present chances to improve our comprehension and regard for regular rhythms. Remote detecting, satellite symbolism, and large information examination give instruments to screen natural changes at a worldwide scale. These advances empower researchers, preservationists, and policymakers to follow shifts in environments, recognize arising dangers, and execute designated mediations to safeguard biodiversity and alleviate the effect of environmental change.

With regards to metropolitan preparation and configuration, consolidating a comprehension of regular rhythms is fundamental for making economical and strong urban areas. Green spaces, metropolitan timberlands, and feasible framework can be intended to impersonate normal biological systems and backing biodiversity. The effect of such plans reaches out past biological advantages to incorporate upgraded personal satisfaction, further developed air and water quality, and expanded strength to environment related difficulties.

According to a worldwide viewpoint, global participation is basic in tending to the difficulties presented by the changing examples of seasons. Transboundary issues like deforestation, overfishing, and environmental change require cooperative endeavors that rise above international limits. Understanding and regarding normal rhythms become bringing together rules that guide countries toward shared objectives of preservation, supportability, and environment flexibility.

At its center, the significance of understanding and regarding regular rhythms is established in a more extensive change in perspective. It requires a change from survey the Earth as an assortment of assets to be taken advantage of to remembering it as a living, interconnected framework that supports all life. The effect of this shift isn't just biological yet additionally stretches out to cultural qualities, monetary frameworks, and administration structures.

Chasing supportable turn of events, strategies and practices that line up with the normal rhythms of the Earth can cultivate a regenerative relationship with the planet. The effect of such a methodology is extraordinary, advancing a comprehensive comprehension of progress that incorporates environmental honesty, social value, and monetary strength. By incorporating the recurrent examples of seasons into dynamic cycles, social orders can push toward a regenerative worldview that supports both the Earth and its occupants.

All in all, the significance of understanding and regarding the normal rhythms implanted in the patterns of the Earth is diverse and extensive. It is an acknowledgment of the significant relationship between human social orders and the climate, a call to adjust our activities to the insight of the planet. The effect of this understanding stretches out from the protection of biodiversity and the relief of environmental change to the advancement of human wellbeing, social lavishness, and supportable turn of events. As stewards of this wondrous planet, it is occupant upon us to embrace and typify the principle.

Chapter 3

Creatures of the Melody

In a domain past the shroud of conventional discernment, where the embroidery of reality winds around itself with strings of sound and repeats reverberate like old murmurs, there exists a spot known as the Symphonious Sanctuary. This ethereal area is home to the mysterious Animals of the Song, creatures whose presence is indivisible from the harmonies and discords that shape the actual texture of their existence.

In this captivated domain, time streams like a waterway, winding its direction through scenes painted with shades of sound. The Animals of the Song, different in structure and pith, possess this steadily evolving ensemble. Some look like agile notes that dance through the air, while others manifest as superb harmonies that reverberate with the principal vibrations of their reality.

At the core of the Consonant Shelter lies the Incomparable Director, a being of massive power and shrewdness who organizes the inestimable songs that oversee the recurring pattern of presence.

The Incomparable Guide's twirly doo, an iridescent wand that appears to draw music from the very air itself, directs the amicable dance of the Animals of the Tune. Each development, each flash of the implement, sends swells through the aural embroidery, molding reality afterward.

In this charmed domain, the idea of language as people comprehend it takes a secondary lounge to the general language of music. The Animals of the Song convey through tunes and harmonies, their feelings and aims woven into the very noticed that penetrate the air. Each being is a living instrument, reverberating with the vibrations of their own extraordinary embodiment, adding to the consistently growing creation of the Consonant Sanctuary.

Among the natives of this otherworldly domain is the Expressive Alarm, an animal whose tune can wind around stories that rise above time itself. With each eerie tune, the Melodious Alarm has the ability to move audience members to far off domains, permitting them to encounter the reverberations of failed to remember stories and untold experiences. The alarm's voice, a magnificent combination of style and crude inclination, charms all who are sufficiently lucky to hear its ethereal tune.

In the shadowed corners of the Symphonious Safe house sneak the Harsh Shadows, puzzling substances that exemplify discord and mayhem. These tricky creatures are the absolute opposite of the amicable tunes that saturate the domain, trying to upset the enormous offset with their chaotic murmurs. The Incomparable Guide, ever cautious, winds around counter-harmonies to contain the impact of the Harsh Shadows, keeping up with the fragile balance that supports the presence of the Consonant Shelter.

As the heavenly songs wind through the air, the Ensemble of Divine Weavers comes into center. These ethereal creatures, looking like brilliant strings of light, explore the flows of the grandiose ensemble with beauty and accuracy. Their motivation is to orchestrate the dissimilar notes of the universe, guaranteeing that the fantastic piece of presence stays a consistent and interconnected embroidery.

In the core of the Symphonious Safe house, there exists the Pleasant Nexus, a union of energy where the songs of the whole domain entwine. The Nexus beats with a dynamic energy, filling in as a point of convergence for the harmonies that radiate from each side of the domain. It is said that the pith of the Consonant Safe house itself dwells inside the Sweet Nexus, a wellspring of vast imagination and imperativeness.

In the domain of the Animals of the Tune, time isn't straight yet rather a liquid continuum where past, present, and future mix in an entrancing dance. The Incomparable Director, with a significant comprehension of the complexities of the enormous tunes, organizes the fleeting ensemble, permitting the inhabitants of the Consonant Sanctuary to explore the flows of time with unrivaled artfulness.

The Consonant Sanctuary isn't without its difficulties, be that as it may. The Dissonant Shadows, with their persistent quest for turmoil, represent a steady danger to the sensitive equilibrium of the domain. The Incomparable Guide, savvy and unflinching, marshals the powers of congruity to face the infringing cacophony, taking part in a ceaseless vast battle to safeguard the holiness of the Symphonious Sanctuary.

At some point, a particular song started to reverberate through the Consonant Sanctuary, a tune that appeared to rise out of the actual soul of the actual domain. The natives, receptive to the subtlest subtleties of the vast ensemble, detected a change in the aural embroidery. The Incomparable Guide, with a wrinkled temple, raised the rod to explore the wellspring of this cryptic song.

As the song unfurled, another substance arose — an encapsulation of crude inventive potential, a Dream of Strange Harmonies. This Dream, brilliant and untamed, had the capacity to produce songs that rose above even the most multifaceted arrangements of the Consonant Asylum. The occupants wondered about the Dream's imaginative ability, attracted to the neglected potential outcomes that resounded in each note.

The Dream of Unfamiliar Harmonies turned into an impetus for change in the Symphonious Safe house, rousing the occupants to investigate new domains of imagination and articulation. The once-natural tunes took on new aspects, developing into harmonies that extended the limits of the occupants' comprehension. The Incomparable Guide, perceiving the Dream's remarkable gift, invited this inundation of innovative energy, meshing it into the consistently growing embroidered artwork of the Symphonious Shelter.

However, with the appearance of the Dream, the Conflicting Shadows detected a chance to take advantage of the weaknesses of the domain. The discordant murmurs became stronger, endeavoring to overwhelm the harmonies that resounded from each corner. The Incomparable Guide, confronted with an extraordinary test, revitalized the natives to remain against the infringing disarray, conjuring the force of solidarity and concordance.

The occupants of the Symphonious Sanctuary, enlivened by the Dream of Unknown Harmonies, joined in an amicable melody that resounded through the domain. The Ensemble of Divine Weavers wove multifaceted examples of light, pushing back the Grating Shadows and reestablishing harmony to the grandiose orchestra. The Dream, remaining at the focal point of the agreeable combination, implanted the domain with an inventive essentialness that rose above the problematic impact of the shadows.

As the enormous battle arrived at its peak, the harmonies of the Consonant Shelter arrived at a crescendo, a radiant articulation of solidarity and flexibility.

The Incomparable Guide, with a grave gesture, recognized the inhabitants' aggregate strength and the Dream's groundbreaking impact. Yet again the domain, washed in agreeable quietness, embraced the strange tunes that had risen up out of the imaginative pot.

The Dream of Unknown Harmonies, having satisfied its motivation, started to blur once more into the embodiment of the Consonant Sanctuary. However, its heritage persevered in the natives' hearts, moving them to keep investigating the unfathomable conceivable outcomes of their imaginative potential. The Incomparable Director, with a look that rose above existence, recognized the steadily changing nature of the vast orchestra, realizing that the tunes of the Symphonious Shelter would proceed to develop and unfurl in manners yet unheard of.

Thus, in the immortal region of the Symphonious Asylum, the occupants proceeded with their amicable presence, directed by the insight of the Incomparable Director and powered by the imaginative soul that the Dream of Strange Harmonies had touched off. The heavenly tunes reverberated through the aural embroidery, winding around a story of solidarity, flexibility, and the interminable quest for strange harmonies.

3.1 Focus on the diverse array of wildlife and their unique contributions to the symphony.

In the core of an immaculate wild, where the air is buzzing with the fragrance of pine and the stir of leaves underneath bunch animals' feet, there exists a dynamic embroidery of life. This safe-haven, immaculate by the infringements of human civilization, overflows with a different cluster of untamed life, every species contributing its interesting voice to the orchestra of nature. Here, the idea of an ensemble takes on a strict importance, as the animals organize an amicable dance that resonates through the old woodlands, reverberating with the rhythms of life.

Among the occupants of this captivated wild are the Murmuring Trees, old sentinels that stand tall and savvy, their branches influencing in the delicate breeze. These lofty creatures act as caretakers of the woods, their leaves stirring with the mysteries of hundreds of years gone by. As the breeze winds through their branches, the Murmuring Trees emanate a delicate song, a demonstration of the insight implanted in their old bark. This woody orchestra frames the underpinning of the wild's living structure.

Underneath the transcending shelter, the Dappled Deer touch calmly, their hooves proceeding with caution on the greenery covered woodland floor. These exquisite animals, decorated with coats that reflect the dappling daylight, move in synchronized designs. The mood of their strides makes a delicate percussion, blending with the melodic murmurs of the trees. The Dappled Deer exemplify the beauty and serenity that saturates the regular orchestra, their presence an artful dance inside the bigger movement of the wild.

In the perfectly clear streams that wander through the core of the wild, the Agreeable Trout explore the ebbs and flows with liquid elegance. Their scales sparkle like glowing notes, getting the daylight as they dart and wind underneath the water's surface. As they swim, the Agreeable Trout produce a sensitive song, a resonating submerged sonata that supplements the stirring leaves and the delicate footfall of the Dappled Deer. The oceanic rhythm turns into a fundamental piece of the wild ensemble, adding a layer of intricacy to the amicable structure.

Above, the Wingsong Birds take off through the sky blue sky, their wings beating in cadenced examples that imitate the ascent and fall of melodic notes. These avian virtuosos make perplexing tunes with their airborne gymnastics, their melodies reverberating through the woodland shelter. Every types of Wingsong Bird contributes an extraordinary tone to the orchestra, from the lilting quavers of the Skylark to the resounding calls of the Songbird. Together, they structure the avian ensemble, winding around an embroidery of song that moves through the treetops.

Settled in the tunnels and hollows of old trees, the Repeating Squirrels add a percussive component to the wild ensemble. Their deft paws drum against the bark, making an enthusiastic musicality that intersperses the surrounding hints of the woodland. As the Repeating Squirrels hasten through the treetops, their musical tricks become a perky contradiction to the more quiet songs of the Murmuring Trees and the Agreeable Trout.

In the midst of the thick underbrush, the Flittering Fireflies arise as glowing notes at night orchestra. Their delicate shine enlightens the dimness, making a heavenly presentation that reflects the stars above. As the Fireflies shudder and dance, their bioluminescent examples produce a visual cadence, adding a mysterious aspect to the hear-able orchestra. The mix of their delicate lights and the melodic soundscape changes the wild into a nighttime wonder, a living creation that proceeds with even without even a trace of daylight.

The Incomparable Howlers, old watchmen of the evening, contribute a profound bass to the orchestra as their frightful calls reverberation through the dimness. These strange animals, hid in the shadows, release base vocalizations that reverberate through the huge scope of the wild. The Incomparable Howlers' commitments add a feeling of profundity and secret to the orchestra, a sign of the untamed and early stage nature of the safe-haven.

In the core of the wild, a magnificent animal known as the Iridescent Wolf wanders. With fur that sparkles like evening glow, the Brilliant Wolf moves with quiet effortlessness, its presence a ghostly tune in the nighttime ensemble. As it lurks through the underbrush, the wolf radiates a symphonious murmur, a special commitment that blends with the encompassing hints of the evening. The Glowing Wolf, an image of the wild's persona, epitomizes the untamed soul that saturates the living ensemble.

The ensemble of the wild isn't simply a hear-able encounter; it is a multisensory festivity of life in the entirety of its structures. The fragrant blooms of the Concordance Blossoms discharge a fragile scent that drifts through the air, mixing with the regular smells of pine and earth. The Concordance Blossoms, with petals that open and close in a musical dance, contribute olfactory notes to the orchestra, making a vivid tactile encounter that enamors all who adventure into the core of the wild.

As the seasons change, so too does the structure of the wild orchestra. The Liquefying Snowflakes, fragile and fleeting, contribute a sharp tinkling as they change into fluid beads during the defrosting of winter. Their transient tunes mark the appearance of spring, a time of restoration and resurrection in the steadily developing ensemble. The moving elements of the wild mirror the back and forth movement of life, an unending rhythm that rises above the limits of time.

Amidst this normal orchestra, the Consonant Agreement Frogs arise during the blustery season. These land and/or water capable virtuosos produce a racket of musical croaks, making an exuberant ensemble that resonates through the damp territories of the wild. The Congruity Frogs' commitments, however apparently turbulent, add an energetic and unusual component to the orchestra, an impression of the immediacy inborn in nature's fabulous sythesis.

The Orchestra of Seasons, a stupendous development inside the wild ensemble, unfurls with the evolving scene. The stirring leaves of pre-winter contribute a melancholic song as they tumble from the branches, making a percussive cadence that denotes the progress to winter. The Murmuring Trees, presently deprived of their foliage, add an unpretentious distress to the ensemble, a piercing sign of the repetitive idea of life in the wild.

As dusks and the stars arise, the Divine Cicadas start their melody. These inestimable bugs, with wings that shine like stardust, produce an infinite murmur that mixes with the nighttime calls of the Incomparable Howlers and the Brilliant Wolf. The Heavenly Cicadas' supernatural commitments hoist the wild orchestra to a vast crescendo, a demonstration of the interconnectedness of the safe-haven with the more extensive divine embroidery.

The occupants of the wild, from the littlest Concordance Blossoms to the most fabulous Murmuring Trees, on the whole make a living ensemble that rises above the limits of individual commitments. Every species, with its exceptional qualities and ways of behaving, adds a layer to the unpredictable creation that characterizes the safe-haven. The ensemble isn't simply an assortment of sounds; it is a cooperative magnum opus, a declaration of the interconnected trap of life that flourishes in the core of the wild.

Amidst this fabulous ensemble, human onlookers become members, their faculties receptive to the subtleties of the regular organization.

The wild, with its heap occupants, turns into a living demonstration of the excellence of biodiversity and the agreeable connections that characterize environments. The occupants of the asylum, each assuming their part in the ensemble, highlight the sensitive equilibrium that supports life in this untamed domain.

As the ensemble of the wild keeps on unfurling, it turns into a living story of the interconnectedness of every single living thing. The stir of leaves, the delicate chatter of streams, the calls of birds, and the frightful tunes of the night all add to an excellent embroidery that recounts the narrative of life in the core of the wild. This orchestra, an immortal magnum opus, fills in as a sign of the significance of saving the holiness of such immaculate sanctuaries, where the congruity of nature can keep on reverberating through the ages.

3.2 Explore the habits, behaviors, and communication methods of different species.

In the core of a sweeping savannah, where the brilliant grasses influence in the cadence of the breeze, a different exhibit of untamed life flourishes. Every species has developed novel propensities, ways of behaving, and specialized strategies that permit them to explore the difficulties of their current circumstance. The many-sided embroidery of life in the savannah is woven with the strings of these particular qualities, making an amicable yet complex environment.

The grand figure of the Savannah Elephant orders consideration as it effortlessly travels through the prairies. These grand animals, with their transcending edges and ivory tusks, display complex social designs. The Savannah Elephants structure very close nuclear families drove by a matron, and their correspondence depends intensely on low-recurrence infrasound, permitting them to pass messages on over tremendous distances. The profound thunders act for of flagging risk, communicating feelings, and planning developments inside the crowd.

Interestingly, the smooth and coordinated Cheetahs, the savannah's quintessential runners, show lone way of behaving. These impressive hunters depend on covertness and speed to chase their prey. The Cheetahs' specialized strategies include a blend of vocalizations, like tweets and snarls, alongside non-verbal communication, including unpredictable tail developments. While they may not shape enormous gatherings like a few different animal categories, Cheetahs convey really to lay out regions and direction with expected mates during the reproducing season.

In the midst of the grasses, the provinces of Meerkats take part in common living. These little, social warm blooded animals cooperate to rummage for food and safeguard their tunnels. Their correspondence is profoundly nuanced, with a different scope of vocalizations, including particular caution calls that caution the gathering of moving toward hunters.

Meerkats likewise utilize visual signs, like stance and tail developments, to pass on data inside the state. This helpful way of behaving guarantees the endurance of the gathering in the difficult savannah climate.

The gymnastic shenanigans of the African Serval add a dash of class to the savannah scene. These slim and spotted cats are talented trackers, utilizing their sharp faculties to distinguish prey in the tall grass. African Servals convey through a mix of vocalizations, including murmurs, murmurs, and twitters, as well as non-vocal signals, for example, looks and body stances. Their wonderful capacity to explore the territory and impart really adds to their prosperity as tricky trackers.

The collective homes of the Friendly Weavers spot the acacia trees, making complicated avian apartment buildings. These little birds are known for their helpful settling conduct, and their perplexing homes act as a demonstration of their social construction. Friendly Weavers utilize various calls and twitters to impart inside the state, organizing exercises, for example, scrounging and alarming each other to likely dangers. The synchronized endeavors of these birds epitomize the advantages of mutual living in the savannah.

In the waterways that cut through the scene, the Hippopotamuses track down shelter. Regardless of their enormous size, these semi-amphibian warm blooded animals are shockingly nimble in water. Correspondence among Hippos includes different vocalizations, from snorts and thunders to blares. These sounds fill various needs, including regional stamping, communicating predominance, and flagging animosity. The Hippopotamus' capacity to convey successfully adds to the foundation and upkeep of social progressive systems inside their units.

On the savannah fields, the transcending Giraffes effortlessly navigate the scene, their long necks going after the delicate leaves at the highest point of acacia trees. These delicate goliaths display both single and social ways of behaving, shaping free affiliations known as pinnacles. Giraffes convey through a scope of vocalizations, including low-recurrence infrasound and grunts, as well as actual prompts, for example, necking, a way of behaving where guys participate in ritualized battle. Their exceptional life structures and ways of behaving grandstand the versatility of life in the savannah.

The complex passages underneath the ground house the tricky Aardvarks, nighttime warm blooded animals that are all around adjusted to tunneling. Aardvarks, with their long noses and strong hooks, convey through a mix of snorts and snuffles, depending on their sharp feeling of smell to explore their underground world. Their lone nature and tunneling propensities make them slippery animals, and their specialized strategies mirror the difficulties and benefits of their nighttime way of life.

In the skies over, the Military Hawks take off with lofty wingspans. These considerable raptors, at the highest point of the savannah's avian ordered progression, display a mix of single and monogamous ways of behaving. Military Hawks convey through clearly, puncturing calls that reverberation across the fields, filling in as regional markers and mating signals. Their amazing hunting ability and ordering presence overhead make them both dreaded and loved by different species in the savannah.

The sweeping savannah is additionally home to the traveling Wildebeests, whose notable relocation designs add to the powerful idea of the environment. Wildebeests structure enormous groups that navigate immense distances looking for crisp touching grounds. Their correspondence includes low snorts and grunts, making a steady mumbling foundation clamor that reverberations across the fields. During relocations, Wildebeests coordinate their developments, displaying the cooperative endeavors of the crowd.

The nighttime trackers of the savannah, the African Lions, rule the night with their strong thunders. These dominant hunters show social way of behaving, framing prides drove by predominant guys. Lions impart through a scope of vocalizations, including thunders that can be heard for a significant distance. These vocalizations effectively lay out regional limits, coordinate hunting procedures, and keep up with social attachment inside the pride. The Lions' great presence and facilitated ways of behaving make them images of solidarity and solidarity in the savannah.

Inside the maze of water channels, the Nile Crocodiles lie on pause, their antiquated heredity going back large number of years. Nile Crocodiles are known for their quiet and patient hunting methodologies, depending on covertness to catch prey. While their correspondence isn't so vocal as a few different animal types, they use nonverbal communication, including posing and tail developments, to convey strength and lay out regions. The Nile Crocodile's capacity to stay unnoticeable and convey unpretentiously highlights its job as a dominant hunter in the oceanic environments of the savannah.

The cooperative connection between the Oxpeckers and huge herbivores adds an interesting dynamic to the savannah's natural web. Oxpeckers, roosted on the backs of Rhinoceroses and different herbivores, act as watchful sentinels, making their hosts aware of the presence of ticks and different parasites. Correspondence among Oxpeckers and their hosts includes a mix of pecking and unmistakable calls, making a mutualistic partnership that benefits the two players. This helpful conduct features the interconnectedness of species in the savannah environment.

In the cool shade of the acacia trees, the Klipspringers explore the rough outcrops with deft nimbleness. These little gazelles, adjusted to the difficult territory, convey through delicate whistles and staccato-like alert calls. Klipspringers' sharp faculties and obscure ways of behaving permit them to explore their rough territories carefully, depending on their specialized strategies to facilitate developments and caution each other to likely dangers.

The savannah's different exhibit of species, each with its remarkable propensities, ways of behaving, and specialized techniques, on the whole winds around the rich embroidered artwork of life in this powerful environment. From the strong thunders of the African Lions to the fragile twitters of the Friendly Weavers, each specie assumes an essential part in keeping up with the sensitive equilibrium of the savannah. The interconnectedness of these ways of behaving highlights the intricacy and versatility of nature's excellent plan, where each string adds to the lively ensemble of life on the savannah fields.

3.3 Emphasize the importance of biodiversity in maintaining the symphonic balance.

In the unpredictable dance of life on The planet, biodiversity arises as a foundation, a unique power that meshes the texture of biological systems into an agreeable ensemble. The extravagance and assortment of living things, each having its exceptional impact in the fabulous piece, add to the flexibility and manageability of our planet. As the sensitive strings of biodiversity join, they structure the unpredictable examples that support the musical equilibrium of nature.

At the core of the biodiversity woven artwork lies the idea of biological reliance, where various species depend on each other for endurance and prosperity. This reliance appears in complex food networks, complicated connections among plants and pollinators, and cooperative unions that have developed over centuries. The interconnectedness of species, each satisfying a particular specialty, is similar to the different instruments in a symphony, each adding its exceptional sound to the general piece.

Consider the lavish spreads of a tropical rainforest, a biodiversity area of interest overflowing with life in heap structures. The transcending covering, with its different cluster of tree species, gives a territory to incalculable living beings. In this orchestra of biodiversity, each tree species contributes its exceptional leaf shapes, compound organizations, and development designs, making microenvironments that help a huge swath of life. From the littlest bugs to the biggest well evolved creatures, the rainforest's biodiversity supports a mind boggling snare of connections, every species assuming a significant part in keeping up with the musical equilibrium.

The significance of biodiversity turns out to be especially obvious in the fertilization dance that happens among blooming plants and their pollinators. Honey bees, butterflies, birds, and different pollinators act as the artists in this orchestra, moving dust starting with one blossom then onto the next as they scrounge for nectar. The outcome isn't just the propagation of plant species however a prospering biological system where the different tunes of blossoming plants blend with the murmur of pollinator movement. The deficiency of any species in this complicated dance undermines the concordance of the whole environment, possibly prompting a fountain of disturbances.

The seas, immense and strange, likewise have an ensemble of biodiversity underneath their waves. Coral reefs, frequently alluded to as the rainforests of the ocean, epitomize the interconnectedness of marine life. Coral polyps, the engineers of these dynamic environments, structure cooperative associations with minuscule green growth, making the staggering exhibit of varieties that describe sound coral reefs. Fish, shellfish, and other marine animals contribute their extraordinary rhythms to this submerged orchestra, every species keeping a sensitive equilibrium in the marine environment.

Think about the dominant hunters of the seas, like sharks. In spite of their fearsome standing, sharks assume a pivotal part in managing the populaces of prey species, forestalling overgrazing and keeping up with the soundness of the marine food web. The expulsion of sharks, frequently because of human exercises, for example, overfishing, upsets the equilibrium of the marine orchestra, prompting flighty outcomes all through the biological system.

The meaning of biodiversity is additionally highlighted in the complex connections among hunter and prey. In African savannahs, the presence of hunters, for example, Lions and Cheetahs shapes the way of behaving and populace elements of herbivores. The touching examples of herbivores, thus, impact the design and arrangement of plant networks. This unique exchange, an indication of biodiversity, guarantees that no single species overwhelms the scene, forestalling environment uneven characters.

The musical equilibrium kept up with by biodiversity stretches out to the tiny domain, where microorganisms assume an essential part in supplement cycling and soil wellbeing. Mycorrhizal organisms structure cooperative relationship with plant roots, working with the trading of supplements and water. Microbes disintegrate natural matter, reusing supplements once more into the environment. These undetectable orchestrators of the dirt ensemble add to the ripeness and versatility of earthly environments.

Human social orders, as well, are complicatedly associated with the ensemble of biodiversity. The variety of plants and creatures that have been tamed for farming structures the groundwork of our food frameworks. Crop variety, for example, guarantees flexibility against bugs and illnesses, giving a cushion against potential yield disappointments. The deficiency of biodiversity in horticultural frameworks, driven by monoculture and the dependence on a couple of staple yields, presents dangers to worldwide food security.

Past unmistakable advantages, biodiversity holds gigantic worth in social and stylish aspects. Native societies all over the planet have kept up with amicable associations with their surroundings for ages, drawing motivation from the assorted greenery that encompass them. The complicated examples of biodiversity track down articulation in craftsmanship, fables, and conventional information, molding the personality of networks and advancing the social embroidered artwork of humankind.

However, regardless of its natural worth and the administrations it gives, biodiversity faces uncommon dangers in the Anthropocene, the age characterized by human effect in the world. Natural surroundings obliteration, contamination, environmental change, over-double-dealing of assets, and obtrusive species by and large add to the disturbing loss of biodiversity on a worldwide scale. The musical equilibrium that has advanced north of millions of years is currently under attack, with results that resound across biological systems and effect human social orders.

The deficiency of biodiversity is similar to the slow blurring of instruments in an ensemble, every vanishing lessening the lavishness and intricacy of the orchestra. At the point when species go wiped out, the extraordinary songs they once contributed are lost until the end of time. The downfall of pollinators, for instance, undermines the propagation of many blossoming plants, upsetting the rhythms of biological systems and jeopardizing the food wellsprings of innumerable organic entities, including people.

In the seas, coral reefs face uncommon difficulties because of climbing ocean temperatures, sea fermentation, and coral fading. The unpredictable dance between coral polyps and their cooperative green growth, a sensitive two part harmony that supports the lively shades of reefs, is upset as corals oust the green growth because of stress. The blurring shades of faded corals represent the delicacy of marine environments despite environmental change and human exercises.

The deficiency of dominant hunters, like wolves in specific biological systems, has prompted flowing impacts on prey populaces and vegetation. Without hunters to direct herbivore numbers, scenes might go through intense changes, influencing the overflow and variety of plant species. The vanishing of cornerstone species, which assume excessively significant parts in biological systems, can set off a cascading type of influence that resounds all through the orchestra of biodiversity.

The effects of biodiversity misfortune stretch out to fundamental biological system benefits that help human prosperity. Timberlands, with their different exhibit of tree species, add to environment guideline by sequestering carbon dioxide. Wetlands channel water, moderate floods, and give natural surroundings to a horde of animal varieties. Biodiversity is the imperceptible director of these biological system administrations, organizing processes that support the circumstances for life on The planet.

Perceiving the direness of the biodiversity emergency, worldwide drives and arrangements intend to address the underlying drivers of biodiversity misfortune and advance preservation endeavors. The Show on Organic Variety, laid out in 1992, fills in as a worldwide system to advance practical turn of events and protection. Targets, for example, the Aichi Biodiversity Targets and the later Post-2020 Worldwide Biodiversity System highlight the requirement for pressing and extraordinary activity to defend biodiversity.

Preservation endeavors, in any case, should go past safeguarding individual species and territories. They should address the fundamental drivers of biodiversity misfortune, including impractical utilization designs, territory obliteration, and environmental change. Economical advancement rehearses that coordinate the protection of biodiversity with human prosperity are critical for accomplishing enduring arrangements.

Safeguarded regions, going from public parks to local area oversaw holds, assume a fundamental part in saving biodiversity. These regions act as safe-havens for different species, giving spaces where biological systems can flourish without the quick tensions of human exercises. In any case, the viability of safeguarded regions relies upon their plan, the executives, and the acknowledgment of the privileges and information on nearby networks.

Notwithstanding safeguarded regions, supportable land-use rehearses, agroecological cultivating strategies, and mindful asset the board add to the preservation of biodiversity. The change to additional feasible and regenerative practices in agribusiness, fisheries, and ranger service can moderate the effects of human exercises on biological systems. By embracing biodiversity-accommodating methodologies, social orders can uphold the flexibility and versatile limit of biological systems.

Schooling and mindfulness are vital parts of biodiversity protection. Encouraging a comprehension of the significance of biodiversity, its part in environment working, and the relationship of species develops a feeling of stewardship among networks. Ecological schooling programs, resident science drives, and associations among analysts and neighborhood networks improve aggregate endeavors to safeguard biodiversity.

Besides, the mix of customary environmental information, frequently held by native and nearby networks, into preservation techniques is fundamental. Native people groups, with their profound associations with the land and its biodiversity, offer important bits of knowledge into feasible asset the executives rehearses. Perceiving and regarding the freedoms of native networks to their domains adds to the protection of biodiversity and the safeguarding of social variety.

Relieving environmental change, a vital driver of biodiversity misfortune, is basic for the fate of biological systems. The decrease of ozone harming substance discharges, the progress to sustainable power sources, and the rebuilding of debased environments all add to environmental change relief and backing the flexibility of biodiversity. The interconnected difficulties of environmental change and biodiversity misfortune require incorporated and composed ways to deal with address the underlying drivers of the two emergencies.

In metropolitan conditions, where human populaces are concentrated, advancing green spaces, supportable metropolitan preparation, and green framework adds to biodiversity protection. Metropolitan environments, however frequently exceptionally altered, can uphold different plant and creature species. By coordinating nature into urban areas, social orders improve the personal satisfaction for occupants and set out open doors for conjunction with assorted types of life.

Eventually, the preservation of biodiversity is a common obligation that requires aggregate activity at neighborhood, public, and worldwide scales. Legislatures, organizations, common society, and people all assume vital parts in cultivating an agreeable relationship with nature. Arrangements that focus on supportability, corporate practices that focus on natural stewardship, and individual decisions that embrace eco-accommodating ways of life add to the insurance of biodiversity.

As mankind faces remarkable difficulties, from the deficiency of biodiversity to environmental change and worldwide pandemics, the significance of biodiversity turns out to be significantly more clear. The orchestra of life, with its heap songs and rhythms, is a demonstration of the interconnectedness of every living thing. The passing of a solitary animal categories, similar to the blurring notes of an instrument, reduces the wealth of the orchestra, influencing the wellbeing and versatility of the whole environment.

In embracing the meaning of biodiversity, social orders have the chance to become stewards of the planet, supporting the fragile strings of life that support all of us. By winding around a story of preservation, reclamation, and maintainable concurrence, we can endeavor to safeguard the mind boggling examples of the biodiversity embroidery. In doing as such, we add to the protection of the World's normal ensemble, guaranteeing that the amicable transaction of species perseveres for a long time into the future.

In the immense and interconnected trap of life on The planet, keeping up with the musical equilibrium of biological systems arises as a basic goal. The idea of environmental equilibrium is much the same as organizing a terrific orchestra, where every species assumes a remarkable part, contributing its tune to the mind boggling structure of nature. From the minute to the glorious, each organic entity in an environment has a section to play in this orchestra, and disturbances to this sensitive concordance can have flowing impacts that resound all through the whole piece.

At the core of keeping up with the musical equilibrium is the comprehension of biodiversity's job in biological systems. Biodiversity, the assortment of life on The planet, includes the various species as well as the hereditary variety inside those species and the variety of environments they occupy. Every species addresses an exceptional note in the ensemble, adding to the lavishness and intricacy of the general structure.

Think about a flourishing tropical rainforest, where the ensemble of biodiversity arrives at its peak. In this verdant domain, a huge number of plant and creature species coincide together as one. The transcending trees structure the foundation of the ensemble, making a complicated overhang that upholds a heap of life structures beneath. From the moment bugs creeping on the woodland floor to the lively birds fluttering through the treetops, every species contributes its exceptional sounds to the instrumental plan.

The job of plants in keeping up with the musical equilibrium couldn't possibly be more significant. Through photosynthesis, plants convert daylight into energy, giving the fundamental notes of the ensemble. The variety of plant species in a rainforest guarantees a steady stockpile of oxygen and supplements, making the circumstances for heap life structures to flourish. As essential makers, plants structure the gauge for the whole environment, supporting herbivores and, thus, carnivores through the exchange of energy up the natural pecking order.

The herbivores in this orchestra, from brushing warm blooded creatures to leaf-chomping bugs, assume a crucial part in forming the construction of plant networks. Their taking care of propensities impact the appropriation and wealth of plant species, keeping any single species from ruling the scene. The musical equilibrium is kept up with as herbivores travel through the environment, forming the sythesis of plant networks and making a unique mosaic of territories.

In the shadows of the rainforest, hunters arise as central members in the ensemble. Pumas, for example, keep up with the equilibrium by managing the populaces of herbivores. Their presence forestalls overgrazing, guaranteeing that plant networks stay different and solid. The ensemble of the rainforest depends on the amicable connections among hunters and prey, keeping any one animal varieties from consuming assets and disturbing the sensitive equilibrium.

The avian tunes of the rainforest add to both the soundscape and the natural elements. Birds, going about as pollinators and seed dispersers, assume pivotal parts in keeping up with plant variety. Their developments through the backwoods convey dust starting with one bloom then onto the next, working with the propagation of plant species. The seeds they consume and later discharge add to the dispersal of vegetation, making new pockets of development and guaranteeing the congruity of the ensemble.

Microorganisms, however frequently unheard in the ensemble, structure the quiet guides of supplement cycling. Microbes and parasites separate natural matter, returning supplements to the dirt and working with the development of plants. This undetectable ensemble of decomposers guarantees that the musical equilibrium is supported by reusing fundamental components, going full circle of life in the rainforest.

The sea-going domains, from freshwater streams to broad seas, additionally have complicated orchestras of biodiversity. Coral reefs, dynamic submerged biological systems, grandstand the relationship of species. Corals, shaping the primary system of the reefs, participate in a harmonious hit the dance floor with minute green growth, giving haven and food as a trade-off for the energy delivered through photosynthesis. The variety of fish, spineless creatures, and other marine living things supplements this coral orchestra, every species adding to the flexibility and strength of the whole environment.

The seas, immense and abounding with life, are controlled by the fragile harmony among hunters and prey. The dominant hunters, like sharks and whales, keep up with the soundness of marine biological systems by controlling the populaces of different species. For example, the presence of sharks forestalls the uncontrolled expansion of specific fish species, protecting the harmony of the maritime orchestra. The complex trap of collaborations guarantees that no single species disturbs the equilibrium, permitting the marine orchestra to resound through the profundities.

The beach front biological systems, where land and ocean meet, are center points of biodiversity and critical for keeping up with the musical equilibrium. Mangroves, with their overly complex roots, give nurseries to fish and go about as cradles against storm floods. The assorted cluster of species, from crabs to birds, adds to the multifaceted creation of these seaside ensembles. Their collaborations, both inside and between environments, feature the interconnectedness that supports the fragile equilibrium of life along the shores.

In the tremendous meadows and savannahs, the ensemble takes on an alternate rhythm. Groups of herbivores, from wildebeests to gazelles, meander the open fields, their developments coordinated by the quest for food and water. The musical equilibrium is kept up with as these herbivores brush in an intelligent way, keeping any single plant species from overwhelming the scene. Their communications with hunters, like lions and cheetahs, make a powerful beat that reverberations across the savannah.

The significance of hunters in keeping up with the musical equilibrium becomes apparent in the idea of trophic fountains. The presence or nonappearance of top hunters can impact the way of behaving of herbivores, which thus influences the vegetation. For instance, without even a trace of hunters, herbivores may overgraze certain plants, prompting a decrease in plant variety. The ensemble depends on the mind boggling connections between species, each note adding to the general piece.

Chapter 4

The Dance of Flora

In the core of a neglected woodland, where the old trees stood like quiet sentinels, their contorted branches coming to towards the sky, there existed a magical domain known exclusively to a picked not many. This ethereal safe-haven, stowed away from according to the unremarkable world, was a sanctuary for animals both supernatural and ordinary, coinciding in a fragile equilibrium.

As the principal beams of the sun punctured through the thick foliage, the backwoods stirred in an orchestra of varieties and sounds. Birds sang tunes that reverberated through the covering, while fragile dewdrops stuck to the leaves, refracting the light in a stunning presentation. The air was loaded up with the powerful fragrance of wildflowers and the hearty smell of the woods floor.

In the midst of this captivated shelter, there flourished a local area of creatures known as the Vegetation. These ethereal substances encapsulated the soul of nature itself, every one a gatekeeper of a particular part of the regular world. From the tallest tree to the littlest sprout, the Vegetation were interlaced with the actual pith of the woodland, their reality a demonstration of the enchanted that pervaded each edge of this secret domain.

The Dance of Vegetation was a holy custom that occurred once consistently, a festival of the repetitive idea of life and the interconnectedness of every living thing. As the selected time moved close to, a tangible energy implanted the air, flagging the impending initiation of the enchanted dance. It was a period of expectation and veneration, as the Vegetation arranged to wind around their unpredictable examples of development and enchantment.

In the core of the woodland, a clearing arose as though by divine plan. The grass in this holy space appeared to shine with a supernatural gleam, and the trees encompassing it stood like quiet observers to the approaching display. As the delegated hour showed up, the Greenery accumulated all around, their brilliant structures making a kaleidoscope of varieties.

At the focal point of the circle stood the Senior Bloom, the most established and savvies of the Greenery. With petals that sparkled with the insight of hundreds of years, the Senior Bloom raised its sensitive ringlets, flagging the start of the Dance of Vegetation. A quiet fell over the gathering as the principal notes of a concealed song consumed the space.

The Verdure moved as a unified whole, their structures influencing like leaves in a delicate breeze. Every development was a demonstration of the novel quintessence they exemplified. The Tree Fairies, with bark-like skin and streaming plant life, established themselves in the earth, their developments slow and consider. The Water Sprites, decorated with beads that shimmered like fluid precious stones, hit the dance floor with a liquid effortlessness that reflected the recurring pattern of streams.

Conversely, the Fire Spirits spun with a power that flashed like blazes, leaving trails of warmth afterward. The Air Nymphs, with translucent wings that got the daylight, took off through the air, their ethereal presence leaving a feeling of weightlessness. Together, they made a living embroidery, an encapsulation of the components in an amicable association.

As the dance unfurled, the enchanted that radiated from the Verdure started to imbue the actual texture of the backwoods. Blossoms sprouted with a recharged dynamic quality, and the actual air appeared to murmur with a concealed energy. The Dance of Verdure was a custom of restoration, a gift from the gatekeepers of the woodland to the land they safeguarded.

With each agile development, the Vegetation discussed with one another as well as with the regular world around them. The old trees influenced in time with the dance, their branches making a church like covering that sifted the daylight into a hypnotizing dappled design. Maybe the whole backwoods had turned into a no nonsense element, throbbing with the energy of the Dance of Greenery.

As the dance arrived at its pinnacle, the Senior Bloom's petals spread out in a presentation of brilliant splendor. A flood of enchantment flowed through the clearing, winding through the greenery the same. The actual embodiment of the timberland appeared to wake up, answering the call of the Verdure. It was a snapshot of greatness, where the limits between the supernatural and the ordinary obscured into a consistent embroidery of presence.

In this elevated condition of association, the Verdure became courses of antiquated astuteness and essential power. The Tree Sprites diverted the strength of the strong oaks, their underlying foundations digging profound into the earth to draw food. The Water Sprites tackled the reviving force of streams and streams, carrying life to the land with each elegant step.

The Fire Spirits, with flares that gleamed in tones of red and gold, summoned the extraordinary energy of fire, refining and restoring. The Air Fairies, with their vaporous developments, conveyed the murmurs of the breeze, distributing seeds and dust to guarantee the ceaseless pattern of development and resurrection.

As the Dance of Greenery approached its decision, a significant feeling of appreciation and concordance encompassed the social event. The Greenery, having satisfied their holy obligation, scattered into the woods, their brilliant structures mixing consistently with the verdure they watched. The clearing, once on fire with sorcery, got back to a quiet tranquility, as though the dance had turned into a vital piece of the timberland's everlasting beat.

In the days that followed, the impacts of the Dance of Greenery waited in the air. The timberland, rejuvenated by the wizardry of the custom, appeared to sparkle with a reestablished imperativeness. Blossoms sprouted with an uncommon splendor, and the tunes of birds reverberated with a recently discovered song. The Dance of Greenery, a brief second in the fantastic embroidery of time, had made a permanent imprint on the core of the woodland.

As the hundreds of years passed, the Dance of Vegetation turned into a murmured legend among the animals of the mysterious domain. Stories of the brilliant creatures who wove enchantment through the actual texture of the backwoods were gone down through ages, turning into a wellspring of motivation and wonderment. The consecrated custom, however interesting, kept on being an image of the persevering through association between the gatekeepers of the timberland and the land they called home.

Thus, in the core of the neglected backwoods, where the old trees stood like quiet sentinels, the Dance of Vegetation remained everlastingly woven into the embroidery of presence. A dance of recharging, of concordance, and of the immortal enchantment that bound the watchmen of the woodland to the land they so savagely secured.

4.1 Examine the role of plants and their intricate dance within the natural symphony.

In the immense ensemble of the normal world, where the components merge in an agreeable orchestra, plants arise as quiet yet significant players, adding to the perplexing dance that shapes the cadence of life on The planet. Established in the dirt and coming to toward the sky, plants exemplify a special and fundamental job in the stupendous embroidery of presence. Their importance stretches out a long ways past the superficial vegetation that meets the eye, diving into the actual texture of environments, environment guideline, and the food of incalculable living things.

At the core of the plant realm's commitment lies the course of photosynthesis, a catalytic dance of daylight, water, and carbon dioxide. Through this mysterious movement, plants saddle the energy of the sun, changing it into the life-supporting power that energizes their development. In doing as such, they support themselves as well as delivery oxygen, an essential gift to the huge number of animals that share the planet. This sensitive trade, frequently disregarded in the hustle of day to day existence, is the foundation of the regular orchestra — a ceaseless compromise that supports the fragile equilibrium of the biosphere.

However, the job of plants stretches out past their apparently static presence. They are the draftsmen of environments, molding scenes and giving territories to a different cluster of living beings. From the transcending shades of old woods to the modest greenery sticking to rocks, plants make specialties and microenvironments that help a shocking assortment of life. This mind boggling dance of vegetation, interlaced and related, structures the premise of biodiversity — the actual embodiment of the World's imperativeness.

Consider the dance of a honey bee as it flutters from one blossom to another, gathering nectar and coincidentally moving dust. This apparently unusual dance is, truth be told, a significant demonstration of fertilization, a fundamental connection in the chain of plant propagation. Through the organization among plants and pollinators, a huge range of natural products, seeds, and blossoms are delivered, guaranteeing the continuation of plant species. It is a dance of mutualistic reliance, a demonstration of the interconnectedness of life.

As plants participate in this dance of propagation, they make a living heritage. Seeds, conveyed by the breeze, scattered by creatures, or covered in the dirt, convey inside them the potential for new life. A dance rises above ages, a movement that has worked out for centuries, adjusting and developing because of the steadily changing elements of the regular world.

The job of plants reaches out into the very air we inhale and the environment that encompasses the planet. The dance of happening, where plants discharge water fume through minuscule pores in their leaves, adds to the arrangement of mists and impacts nearby and worldwide weather conditions.

Backwoods, going about as huge repositories of carbon, assume a vital part in relieving environmental change by engrossing and putting away air carbon dioxide. The complex dance of vegetation, with its extensive results, highlights the sensitive harmony that supports the World's environments.

In investigating the job of plants, it becomes apparent that their dance isn't restricted to the noticeable domain. Underneath the surface, stowed away from relaxed perception, establishes take part in a complicated expressive dance, looking for supplements, water, and steadiness. This underground movement is a quiet power that anchors plants to the earth, giving the establishment to their vertical reach toward daylight. The cooperative connections among plants and mycorrhizal growths, complex associations woven over ages, upgrade supplement take-up and encourage flexibility even with ecological difficulties.

The dance of plants is likewise a demonstration of their versatility. From the strong succulents that flourish in bone-dry deserts to the versatile greeneries gripping to rocks in brutal high conditions, plants have advanced to overcome assorted territories. Their capacity to answer natural signals, from the changing seasons to shifts in temperature and precipitation, mirrors a powerful dance of endurance and variation that has unfurled over geographical ages.

In the unpredictable movement of the plant realm, certain species stand apart as trailblazers, pushing the limits of what appears to be conceivable. Consider the versatile seeds that lie lethargic for years, even many years, trusting that the ideal second will develop. These natural people who jump through time are essential for a dance that traverses ages, permitting plants to recolonize upset scenes and revive regions once considered cold.

The dance of plants, in any case, isn't without its difficulties. In a world formed by human exercises, the sensitive equilibrium of nature is frequently disturbed. Deforestation, living space obliteration, contamination, and environmental change present considerable dangers to vegetation and, likewise, the unpredictable dance of the regular ensemble. As species face the unsafe dance of endurance despite anthropogenic tensions, the requirement for protection and maintainable practices turns out to be perpetually earnest.

Endeavors to comprehend and safeguard the dance of plants include logical request as well as a significant appreciation for the inborn worth of biodiversity. Protection drives plan to save individual species as well as the complicated collaborations and connections that structure the natural embroidered artwork. The job of plants, as designers of environments and watchmen of biodiversity, turns into a mobilizing point for those focused on shielding the planet's normal legacy.

In gardens and developed scenes, people participate in a harmonious hit the dance floor with plants, developing assortments that act as wellsprings of food, medication, and stylish joy.

Horticulture, an old partnership among humankind and plants, addresses a cognizant work to tackle the abundance of the normal world. However, the difficulties of present day agribusiness, set apart by monoculture, substance inputs, and unreasonable practices, highlight the significance of rethinking our relationship with the plant realm.

Chasing manageable conjunction, the standards of agroecology and regenerative agribusiness arise as directing reference points. These methodologies look to emulate the many-sided dance of regular biological systems, advancing biodiversity, soil well-being, and flexibility. The dance of plants, when directed by the rhythms of nature, finds reverberation in these comprehensive methodologies that perceive the interconnectedness of soil, plants, creatures, and people.

In the domain of human wellbeing, the dance of plants becomes the dominant focal point as customary medication and home grown cures draw upon the restorative properties of different plant species. The information went down through ages, frequently established in native insight, verifies the significant connection among people and the plant realm. The dance of mending, a delicate influence between plant cures and the human body's unpredictable frameworks, keeps on being a basic piece of all encompassing prosperity.

The plant realm's dance broadens its impact into social and profound aspects. Across human advancements and ages, plants have been worshipped as images of life, recovery, and amazing quality. Hallowed forests, old trees, and restorative spices become central places of customs and functions, epitomizing an association between the earthbound and the heavenly. The dance of plants, in this unique situation, turns into a dance of respect, a festival of the significant exchange among humankind and the normal world.

In the contemporary period, as social orders wrestle with ecological difficulties and look for economical pathways forward, the dance of plants takes on recharged importance. Protection endeavors, reforestation drives, and the advancement of green spaces inside metropolitan scenes mirror a developing familiarity with the crucial job plants play in keeping up with environmental equilibrium. The direness of moderating environmental change and protecting biodiversity highlights the requirement for an aggregate obligation to encouraging an agreeable dance among people and the plant realm.

Schooling turns into an essential instrument in developing an appreciation for the dance of plants. From youth to cutting edge logical investigations, understanding the complexities of vegetation encourages biological proficiency and an ethic of stewardship. Professional flowerbeds, nature holds, and instructive projects become fields where the dance of plants is displayed, welcoming individuals to wonder about the variety, excellence, and versatility of the plant realm.

All in all, the job of plants and their mind boggling dance inside the regular orchestra is a story woven into the actual texture of life on The planet. From the tiny dance of atoms inside chloroplasts to the amazing expressive dance of biological systems spreading over landmasses, plants shape the world in significant ways. Their dance is one of food, propagation, transformation, and flexibility — a movement that rises above time and associates generally living things in a snare of reliance.

As humankind wrestles with the difficulties of the cutting edge world, the dance of plants entices as a wellspring of motivation and direction. In perceiving the intrinsic worth of biodiversity, embracing supportable practices, and encouraging a profound veneration for the normal world, people can adjust their moves toward the immortal dance of plants. The ensemble of life, with plants as its instrumental spine, welcomes us to join the dance — a dance of conjunction, concordance, and a common excursion on this phenomenal planet we call home.

4.2 Discuss the symbiotic relationships between plants and other organisms.

In the mind boggling trap of life that covers the Earth, cooperative connections among plants and different creatures stand as demonstration of the interconnectedness and relationship of the regular world. From minute cooperations in the dirt to complex organizations between transcending trees and heap animals, these harmonious moves shape environments, impact biodiversity, and add to the flexibility of life on our planet.

At the base of numerous advantageous connections lies the interesting coalition among plants and mycorrhizal growths. Underneath the dirt's surface, these mycorrhizal affiliations structure a mind boggling network that works with supplement trade among growths and plant roots. The growths, with their string like designs called hyphae, stretch out a long ways past the range of plant roots, successfully extending the plant's ability to get to water and supplements like phosphorus and nitrogen. Consequently, the plant gives the parasites carbs created through photosynthesis.

This mutualistic dance among plants and mycorrhizal parasites isn't just a demonstration of their coevolution yet additionally a critical calculate the wellbeing and imperativeness of earthly environments. It empowers plants to flourish in supplement unfortunate soils and adds to the general flexibility of biological systems notwithstanding ecological difficulties. The mycorrhizal network, frequently alluded to as the "Wood Wide Web," embodies the covered up, interconnected world underneath our feet that assumes a critical part in supporting life over the ground.

Over the dirt surface, the dance of fertilization unfurls — a staggering presentation of participation among plants and their pollinators. Honey bees, butterflies, birds, bats, and, surprisingly, the breeze act as fundamental accomplices in this perplexing movement.

As pollinators look for nectar and gather dust, they incidentally work with the exchange of dust starting with one bloom then onto the next, empowering treatment and the development of seeds. This organization is a foundation of plant generation and assumes an essential part in keeping up with biodiversity.

Consider the dance between blossoming plants and honey bees, a relationship that has developed more than large number of years. Blossoms, embellished with energetic varieties and sweet scents, draw in honey bees looking for sustenance. As honey bees dig into the blooms to gather nectar, dust grains stick to their bodies. At the point when these honey bees visit another blossom, a portion of the dust is moved, prompting cross-fertilization and hereditary variety among plant populaces. This coevolutionary dance guarantees the conceptive progress of the two plants and pollinators.

The complexities of fertilization reach out past the domain of honey bees to incorporate a variety of particular associations. Hummingbirds, with their long bills and concentrated tongues, are attracted to rounded blossoms, while butterflies, with their sensitive vacillating flight, are frequently connected with open, brilliantly shaded sprouts. Indeed, even nighttime pollinators, like moths and bats, add to the fertilization dance, each assuming an extraordinary part in the orchestra of regenerative achievement.

Past the domain of noticeable pollinators, the breeze likewise partakes in the dance, especially on account of plants that depend on anemophily — a type of fertilization where the breeze conveys dust starting with one bloom then onto the next. Grasses, many trees, and certain blossoming plants have advanced to deliver bountiful measures of lightweight, airborne dust, exploiting the breeze's capacity to scatter these regenerative particles over extensive distances.

In oceanic biological systems, an alternate however similarly imperative dance happens among plants and sea-going organic entities. Lowered plants in freshwater conditions structure organizations with different life forms, including green growth, microbes, and spineless creatures. These connections add to the wellbeing and soundness of amphibian environments, advancing water lucidity, supplement cycling, and natural surroundings variety.

One momentous illustration of a cooperative relationship in oceanic conditions is the relationship between specific plants and nitrogen-fixing microorganisms. In particular designs called knobs on the plant's underlying foundations, these microbes convert air nitrogen into a structure that the plant can use for development. Consequently, the plant furnishes the microscopic organisms with starches. This nitrogen-fixing dance is critical in supplement unfortunate sea-going natural surroundings, where it upgrades the accessibility of nitrogen — a crucial supplement for plant development.

As the dance of advantageous interaction reaches out into earthly biological systems, another captivating organization arises: that among plants and creatures as mutualistic connections. Subterranean insects, for instance, take part in mutualistic collaborations with specific plants through a cycle known as myrmecochory. In this harmonious dance, subterranean insects gather and scatter seeds, frequently putting away them in underground loads. The seeds, outfitted with members alluring to subterranean insects, tempt the bugs to convey them to new areas. This dispersal procedure benefits the two players — the plants gain a benefit in seed circulation, and the insects get a prize as supplement rich designs connected to the seeds.

Also, the dance among plants and herbivores uncovers complicated biological equilibriums. While certain herbivores consume plant material, others lay out advantageous connections that benefit the two players. On account of specific bugs and plants, herbivores might sequester substance compounds from the plants, involving them as a safeguard system against hunters. This mutualistic dance makes a sensitive balance, where herbivores gain security, and plants benefit from diminished predation pressure.

In the stupendous embroidered artwork of rainforests, where biodiversity arrives at amazing levels, the dance of mutualism is on full presentation. Epiphytic plants, like orchids and bromeliads, frequently track down help on the parts of tall trees, using them as hosts. Consequently, these epiphytes add to the general variety of the biological system, giving environments to bugs, frogs, and different organic entities. The perplexing dance among epiphytes and their host trees epitomizes the multi-layered connections that portray different biological systems.

A remarkable illustration of mutualism in rainforests includes the relationship between specific plants and insects. Acacia plants, for example, have developed particular designs called "domatia" that give safe house and food to subterranean insects. Consequently, the subterranean insects guard the acacia plants against herbivores and contending vegetation. This mutualistic dance helps the acacia plants as well as impacts the design and elements of the whole environment.

As we investigate the universe of oceanic and earthly cooperative connections, the dance reaches out into the microbial domain. The rhizosphere, the dirt locale straightforwardly impacted by plant roots, is a clamoring field where plants participate in unpredictable organizations with a bunch of microorganisms. Microbes and parasites structure unions with plant roots, adding to supplement cycling, sickness obstruction, and generally speaking plant wellbeing.

Quite possibly of the most celebrated advantageous relationship in the microbial world is the mycorrhizal affiliation referenced before.

This organization among plants and parasites upgrades supplement take-up, advances soil structure, and adds to the general strength of biological systems. Notwithstanding mycorrhizae, other helpful soil organisms, for example, nitrogen-fixing microbes and phosphate-solubilizing microorganisms, participate in advantageous hits the dance floor with plants, working with supplement obtaining and advancing plant development.

In rural frameworks, understanding and bridling these cooperative connections have significant ramifications for maintainable practices. The utilization of mycorrhizal inoculants, cover yields, and harvest turns means to upgrade the helpful communications among plants and soil organisms. By encouraging advantageous connections, ranchers can work on supplement accessibility, lessen the requirement for substance inputs, and advance the general wellbeing of rural biological systems.

In the realm of sea-going beneficial interaction, coral reefs stand as lively environments that epitomize unpredictable organizations. Corals, little creatures having a place with the phylum Cnidaria, structure cooperative associations with photosynthetic green growth known as zooxanthellae. The corals give a safeguarded climate and inorganic supplements for the green growth, while the green growth contribute sugars and oxygen through photosynthesis. This mutualistic dance is the underpinning of coral reef environments, supporting a stunning variety of marine life.

In the profundities of the sea, aqueous vent environments feature one more element of advantageous connections. Monster tube worms, for instance, structure organizations with chemosynthetic microorganisms inside their tissues. These microorganisms use synthetic substances radiating from the aqueous vents to create natural mixtures, giving food to the cylinder worms. This dance in the profound sea, absent any trace of daylight, shows life's versatility and the noteworthy variety of cooperative organizations.

While numerous cooperative connections are gainful together, some include a parasitic accomplice that takes advantage of the host living being. Parasitic plants, for example, get supplements from their host plants, frequently to the disservice of the host's wellbeing. Dodder, a parasitic plant with string like stems, twines around the host plant, laying out vascular associations with extricate water and supplements. In spite of the fact that parasitism is a type of beneficial interaction, it contrasts from mutualism in that one accomplice benefits to the detriment of the other.

On account of parasitic organisms, for example, rusts and mucks, the relationship with plants can be adverse. These growths cause illnesses in different plant species, influencing agrarian yields and normal environments. The dance between parasitic growths and plants turns into a battle for endurance, where the organisms exploit the plants for their own regenerative achievement, frequently prompting financial misfortunes and natural lopsided characteristics.

In spite of the difficulties presented by parasitism, most of cooperative connections in nature are described by mutualistic collaborations. These associations add to the dependability and versatility of environments, upgrade supplement cycling, and encourage biodiversity. The dance among plants and their cooperative accomplices, whether infinitesimal parasites or charming pollinators, highlights the perplexing snare of life that supports the biosphere.

As human exercises keep on affecting the planet, understanding and valuing advantageous connections become basic for protection and maintainable practices. Protection endeavors that focus on the safeguarding of key harmonious communications, for example, fertilization organizations and mycorrhizal affiliations, add to the general wellbeing of environments. Furthermore, recognizing the worth of biodiversity in the entirety of its structures supports the significance of safeguarding the complicated moves that shape the regular world.

All in all, the cooperative connections among plants and different living beings structure the strings of an immense embroidery that wraps the Earth. From the minuscule unions in the dirt to the appealling associations between blossoming plants and pollinators, these cooperative moves shape environments, impact biodiversity, and add to the strength of life on our planet. As we disentangle the complexities of these connections, we gain understanding into the sensitive adjusts that support the biosphere — a movement of relationship, collaboration, and mutualistic correspondence that characterizes the dance of life on The planet.

4.3 Highlight the significance of plant life in sustaining ecosystems.

In the mind boggling mosaic of life that covers the Earth, vegetation arises as a major foundation, assuming a urgent part in supporting biological systems across the globe. From the transcending shelters of rainforests to the versatile bushes of bone-dry deserts, plants, with their different structures and works, contribute essentially to the equilibrium and imperativeness of the regular world. The meaning of vegetation in supporting environments stretches out a long ways past their stylish magnificence; it envelops basic natural capabilities, biodiversity support, environment guideline, and the arrangement of fundamental assets for heap creatures.

One of the essential commitments of plants to environment food lies in their job as essential makers. Through the course of photosynthesis, plants bridle the energy of daylight to change over carbon dioxide and water into natural mixtures, principally sugars. This essential speculative chemistry not just energizes the development and advancement of the actual plants yet in addition frames the bedrock of the well established pecking order. Herbivores, thus, consume plant matter, starting a fountain of energy move through progressive trophic levels.

The complicated dance of hunter prey connections that results is subject to the overflow and strength of plant networks. Carnivores, omnivores, and foragers all infer their food straightforwardly or in a roundabout way from plant-determined energy.

This reliance shapes the premise of food networks, many-sided organizations of taking care of connections that characterize the progression of energy and supplements inside biological systems. Consequently, the meaning of vegetation in supporting biological systems isn't bound to their nearby environmental factors however swells through whole biotic networks.

Also, vegetation adds to the creation and upkeep of natural surroundings that help different collections of organic entities. Backwoods, meadows, wetlands, and coral reefs are instances of environments molded by the particular qualities of their plant networks. The complicated design of a timberland, for example, gives specialties to a large number of organic entities, from bugs staying in the leaf litter to birds settling in the covering. The rich biodiversity of such territories is a demonstration of the basic job of plants in molding and supporting biological systems.

Inside these environments, the variety of plant species further upgrades biological versatility. Monoculture, the development of a solitary plant animal groups over enormous regions, might be useful in horticulture yet misses the mark on flexibility that different plant networks proposition to normal environments. Conversely, biological systems with an assortment of plant animal categories are better prepared to endure natural variances, oppose infections, and adjust to evolving conditions. The complicated transaction of different vegetation goes about as a support against unsettling influences, adding to the soundness and life span of biological systems.

Biodiversity, complicatedly connected with the soundness of biological systems, is cultivated by the fluctuated structures and elements of vegetation. Each plant species possesses an exceptional natural specialty, connecting with explicit living beings and answering particular ecological circumstances. This variety of characteristics and transformations upgrades the general versatility of biological systems, permitting them to weather conditions moves going from climatic varieties to the development of new nuisances or illnesses.

Past their biological capabilities, plants assume a critical part in controlling environment designs on both nearby and worldwide scales. The course of happening, where plants discharge water fume through small pores in their leaves, adds to the arrangement of mists and impacts neighborhood weather conditions. Woods, specifically, go about as huge environment controllers through the retention and arrival of carbon dioxide.

In the continuous fight against environmental change, plants arise as strong partners in sequestering carbon — a cycle basic to moderating the ascent in barometrical carbon dioxide levels. Woods, frequently alluded to as the "lungs of the Earth," retain carbon dioxide during photosynthesis, putting away it in their biomass and in the dirt. This aides in controlling worldwide environment as well as adds to the anticipation of additional biodiversity misfortune and the security of imperative biological system administrations.

Also, plants work with supplement cycling inside biological systems, one more key part of their job in supporting life. Fallen leaves, twigs, and other natural matter are separated by decomposers, like growths and microbes, delivering fundamental supplements once more into the dirt. This supplement cycling is fundamental for the wellbeing and efficiency of environments, giving the structure blocks to new establish development and supporting the wholesome necessities of different living beings inside the food web.

The mind boggling connections among plants and soil microorganisms further improve supplement accessibility. Mycorrhizal organisms structure harmonious relationship with plant roots, expanding their scope and supporting the retention of supplements, especially phosphorus. Consequently, plants furnish these organisms with sugars created through photosynthesis. This underground dance of mutualistic cooperations adds to the general supplement elements of biological systems, guaranteeing the supported fruitfulness of soils.

Plants additionally go about as engineers of scenes, impacting geographical cycles and molding the actual qualities of environments. The foundations of plants settle soil, forestalling disintegration and avalanches. Mangroves and waterfront vegetation act as normal cradles against storm floods, shielding seaside networks from the attacks of outrageous climate occasions. The powerful transaction between vegetation and the actual climate represents their job as environment engineers, molding living spaces and impacting the versatility of scenes.

In freshwater environments, amphibian plants contribute altogether to water quality and natural surroundings structure. Lowered amphibian plants give haven to fish and spineless creatures, while drifting plants make concealed regions that assist with directing water temperature. Furthermore, the complex root foundations of sea-going plants assume a part in supplement cycling, retaining overabundance supplements and forestalling water contamination. The strength of amphibian environments, from lakes to streams, is unpredictably connected to the presence and wealth of oceanic vegetation.

The meaning of vegetation in supporting environments is especially clear in the delicate yet biodiverse domains of wetlands. Wetlands go about as normal channels, cleaning water by catching dregs and supplement toxins. The thick vegetation of wetlands, including emanant plants and drifting species, assumes a urgent part in keeping up with water quality and supporting a rich cluster of sea-going and earthbound life. As crucial nurseries for some species, wetlands add to the general soundness of adjoining environments, filling in as irreplaceable repositories of biodiversity.

In desert biological systems, where brutal circumstances win, the versatility of vegetation is displayed as succulents, xerophytes, and different variations that empower plants to flourish in dry conditions.

The interesting elements of desert plants, for example, water-putting away tissues and decreased leaf surfaces, represent their capacity to explore water shortage. Besides, these variations add to the general biodiversity and natural elements of deserts, where vegetation gives food and territory to various specific life forms.

The connection between vegetation and creatures, both in earthbound and oceanic biological systems, features the relationship that portrays the regular world. For herbivores, plants are a wellspring of food as well as a driver of conduct transformations and developmental cycles. Thus, carnivores and omnivores are complicatedly connected to herbivores in complex hunter prey elements. The soundness of plant populaces impacts the overflow and variety of herbivores, making way for flowing impacts all through the food web.

The coevolutionary dance among plants and herbivores frequently prompts the improvement of safeguard components, for example, synthetic mixtures and actual designs, in light of herbivore pressure. This unpredictable weapons contest shapes the attributes of plant networks and adds to the general strength and flexibility of biological systems. The sensitive harmony among herbivores and plants, interceded by biological variables, makes dynamic scenes where species advance working together with their current circumstance.

In marine environments, the connection between vegetation and marine organic entities takes on novel aspects. Coral reefs, frequently alluded to as the rainforests of the ocean, embody the advantageous dance among corals and photosynthetic green growth. The corals give a substrate to the green growth, while the green growth, through photosynthesis, produce oxygen and natural mixtures that sustain the corals. This mutualistic relationship is the groundwork of coral reef biological systems, supporting a stunning exhibit of marine life.

Additionally, the perplexing dance between marine plants, like seagrasses and kelp, and marine organic entities adds to the extravagance and intricacy of beach front environments. Seagrasses give territories to various species, including fish, scavangers, and mollusks, while kelp woods establish three-layered conditions that harbor assorted networks. The soundness of these marine biological systems, indispensable for fisheries and beach front biodiversity, is unpredictably connected to the presence and wealth of vegetation.

The meaning of vegetation in supporting environments turns out to be especially strong even with progressing worldwide difficulties, including environmental change, territory misfortune, and biodiversity decline. Environmental change, driven by human exercises, represents a danger to establish networks around the world. Changed precipitation designs, climbing temperatures, and outrageous climate occasions can disturb the fragile equilibrium of biological systems, affecting the appropriation and overflow of plant species.

The results of environmental change stretch out past individual plant species to whole biological systems. Changes in plant disseminations can influence the creation of networks, adjust food networks, and effect the accessibility of assets for different living beings. In the Icy, for instance, the infringement of woody bushes into generally herbaceous tundra environments is modifying the living space for transient herbivores and changing the elements of the whole biological system.

Living space misfortune, driven by human exercises, for example, deforestation and urbanization, represents an immediate danger to vegetation and, likewise, to the heap creatures that rely upon these natural surroundings. As regular scenes are switched over completely to agribusiness, metropolitan regions, or modern zones, the unpredictable dance of species collaborations is upset, prompting decreases in biodiversity and the deficiency of biological system administrations. Preservation endeavors pointed toward saving normal living spaces and reestablishing debased scenes are fundamental for keeping up with the biological capabilities given by vegetation.

Biodiversity misfortune, a result of environment obliteration, overexploitation, and other anthropogenic elements, further highlights the earnestness of safeguarding plant networks. The eradication of plant species, whether through direct abuse or aberrant outcomes of ecological change, can significantly affect biological systems. Each lost species addresses a string eliminated from the perplexing embroidery of life, possibly unwinding the sensitive equilibrium that supports environments.

Preservation drives, accordingly, progressively center around saving individual plant species as well as the complex cooperations and connections that describe biological systems. Safeguarded regions, professional flowerbeds, and territory reclamation projects become basic apparatuses in shielding plant variety and the biological capabilities related with it. Besides, the mix of customary biological information and native practices adds to all encompassing methodologies that perceive the natural worth of vegetation in supporting environments.

In the domain of farming, the meaning of vegetation is similarly fundamental. Crop plants, the groundwork of worldwide food frameworks, are the consequence of centuries of taming and specific reproducing. The Green Transformation, set apart by the inescapable reception of high-yielding harvest assortments and concentrated rural practices, has added to expanded food creation yet additionally raised worries about ecological supportability and biodiversity misfortune.

A shift toward supportable farming, embracing agroecological standards, tries to accommodate the requirements of food creation with the conservation of biodiversity and biological system wellbeing. Agroforestry, cover editing, and coordinated bother the board are among the practices that perceive the significance of plant variety in keeping up with soil fruitfulness, improving flexibility, and supporting helpful organic entities.

By adjusting farming practices to environmental standards, it becomes conceivable to bridle the meaning of vegetation in supporting biological systems as well as the worldwide human populace.

Instructive drives assume a crucial part in cultivating a comprehension of the meaning of vegetation in supporting environments. From youth to cutting edge examinations in biology and ecological science, finding out about the many-sided connections among plants and their surroundings imparts an appreciation for the intricacies of the normal world. Greenhouses, nature saves, and instructive projects become roads for investigating the different structures and elements of vegetation, underscoring their job as designers of environments.

All in all, the meaning of vegetation in supporting biological systems is woven into the actual texture of life on The planet. From their central job as essential makers to their effect on environment designs, living space creation, and biodiversity support, plants shape the perplexing moves that portray biological systems. The fragile transaction among plants and different organic entities, from minuscule associations in the dirt to complex connections in assorted biological systems, highlights the interconnectedness of all life. As mankind explores the difficulties of the Anthropocene, perceiving and regarding the significance of vegetation becomes basic for cultivating an agreeable conjunction with the normal world.

Vegetation, an apparently static presence in the regular world, arises as a powerful power that supports the many-sided dance of life inside environments. From the microcosmic connections in the dirt to the terrific embroidery of timberlands and prairies, the meaning of vegetation in supporting environments is diverse and basic to the equilibrium and versatility of the biosphere.

At the core of this environmental artful dance is the course of photosynthesis, an essential speculative chemistry that changes daylight, carbon dioxide, and water into the natural mixtures that fuel plant development. As essential makers, plants start the progression of energy through biological systems, giving food to herbivores and making way for the intricate trap of hunter prey communications that portrays food networks. This essential job in energy move lays out plants as the backbone of environments, molding the accessibility of assets for the bunch creatures that rely upon them.

The unique connections among plants and herbivores structure a focal story in the food of biological systems. Herbivores, going from bugs to huge well evolved creatures, assume an essential part in managing plant populaces and molding local area structure. The particular tension applied by herbivores has prompted the advancement of different protection components in plants, from synthetic mixtures that discourage taking care of to actual designs that limit herbivore access. This coevolutionary dance, molded by natural associations, impacts the dispersion and overflow of plant species, adding to the biodiversity and security of biological systems.

Besides, the complicated connections stretch out past herbivores to envelop carnivores, omnivores, and foragers in a mind boggling trap of trophic communications. The strength of plant populaces impacts the overflow and variety of herbivores, making way for flowing impacts all through the food web. Hunter prey connections, directed by the accessibility of plant assets, make a sensitive equilibrium that shapes the elements of environments. The meaning of vegetation in supporting environments is in this way complicatedly connected to the biodiversity and strength of these mind boggling snare of life.

The design and sythesis of plant networks add to the creation and upkeep of environments, molding the scenes that help different collections of organic entities. Backwoods, meadows, wetlands, and coral reefs are models of environments molded by the particular attributes of their plant networks. The mind boggling dance of various plant species inside these territories gives specialties and microenvironments to a huge number of creatures, from microorganisms in the dirt to birds in the covering.

Inside these environments, the variety of plant species further improves biological strength. Monoculture, the development of a solitary plant animal categories over huge regions, might be useful in farming yet misses the mark on versatility that different plant networks proposition to regular biological systems. Interestingly, biological systems with an assortment of plant animal categories are better prepared to endure ecological variances, oppose illnesses, and adjust to evolving conditions. The perplexing transaction of different vegetation goes about as a cradle against unsettling influences, adding to the dependability and life span of environments.

Besides, the meaning of vegetation in supporting environments reaches out into the domain of supplement cycling — a urgent part of biological system capability. Fallen leaves, twigs, and other natural matter from plants are separated by decomposers, like parasites and microbes, delivering fundamental supplements once again into the dirt. This supplement cycling is fundamental for the wellbeing and efficiency of environments, giving the structure blocks to new establish development and supporting the nourishing necessities of different creatures inside the food web.

The perplexing connections among plants and soil microorganisms further upgrade supplement accessibility. Mycorrhizal growths, framing advantageous relationship with plant roots, expand their scope and help in the retention of supplements, especially phosphorus. Consequently, plants furnish these organisms with sugars delivered through photosynthesis. This underground dance of mutualistic collaborations adds to the general supplement elements of environments, guaranteeing the supported ripeness of soils.

The effect of vegetation on environment guideline highlights its worldwide importance. The course of happening, where plants discharge water fume through minuscule pores in their leaves, adds to the development of mists and impacts nearby weather conditions.

Backwoods, with their thick shelters, go about as huge environment controllers through the ingestion and arrival of carbon dioxide. The job of plants in relieving environmental change is additionally exemplified by their capacity to sequester carbon — a crucial cycle for settling climatic carbon dioxide levels and forestalling further biodiversity misfortune.

Woodlands, frequently alluded to as the "lungs of the Earth," retain carbon dioxide during photosynthesis, putting away it in their biomass and in the dirt. This aides in directing worldwide environment as well as adds to the avoidance of additional biodiversity misfortune and the security of fundamental biological system administrations. The interconnectedness of vegetation, environment guideline, and biodiversity highlights the worldwide ramifications of saving and reestablishing plant biological systems.

Amphibian biological systems, from freshwater bodies to marine conditions, feature the different jobs of vegetation in supporting life underneath the surface. Lowered oceanic plants in freshwater conditions give natural surroundings, food, and shelter for different living beings, including fish, spineless creatures, and creatures of land and water. The complicated dance of oceanic plant networks adds to water quality, oxygenation, and supplement cycling, forming the elements of these fundamental environments.

In marine conditions, the cooperative connection among corals and photosynthetic green growth, known as zooxanthellae, is a key part in the food of coral reef environments. Corals give a substrate to the green growth, while the green growth, through photosynthesis, produce oxygen and natural mixtures that sustain the corals. This mutualistic dance is the underpinning of coral reef environments, supporting a stunning exhibit of marine life and adding to the general biodiversity of the seas.

Moreover, wetlands, frequently ignored yet naturally rich biological systems, represent the meaning of vegetation in supporting remarkable territories. Wetlands go about as regular channels, purging water by catching dregs and supplement toxins. The thick vegetation of wetlands, including rising plants and drifting species, assumes an essential part in keeping up with water quality and supporting a rich cluster of oceanic and earthbound life. As essential nurseries for some species, wetlands add to the general strength of nearby biological systems, filling in as fundamental supplies of biodiversity.

The strength of vegetation is especially clear in parched conditions, where transformations, for example, deliciousness and dry spell resilience permit plants to flourish in water-scant circumstances. The remarkable elements of desert plants add to the general biodiversity and biological elements of dry environments, where vegetation gives food and territory to different particular organic entities. The complex dance of life in deserts grandstands the capacity of plants to adjust to outrageous circumstances and highlights their part in supporting life in assorted conditions.

The meaning of vegetation in supporting environments isn't without its difficulties, particularly in that frame of mind of anthropogenic exercises. Environment misfortune, driven by deforestation, urbanization, and farming extension, represents an immediate danger to establish biological systems and the biodiversity they support. As normal scenes are switched over completely to human-ruled spaces, the complicated dance of species communications is disturbed, prompting decreases in biodiversity and the deficiency of basic biological system administrations.

Biodiversity misfortune, a result of territory obliteration, overexploitation, and environmental change, further highlights the desperation of safeguarding plant biological systems. Each lost plant species addresses a string eliminated from the perplexing embroidery of life, possibly disentangling the fragile equilibrium that supports biological systems. Preservation endeavors pointed toward saving individual plant species as well as the many-sided communications and connections that describe environments become basic for keeping up with the natural capabilities given by vegetation.

In the horticultural domain, where human reliance on plant assets is significant, the meaning of vegetation takes on extra aspects. Crop plants, trained and developed for food, fiber, and different items, address a demonstration of the coevolutionary connection among people and plants. The Green Upset, set apart by the inescapable reception of high-yielding harvest assortments and serious farming practices, has essentially expanded worldwide food creation yet additionally raised worries about ecological supportability, biodiversity misfortune, and the effect on biological systems.

Practical horticulture, grounded in agroecological standards, looks to accommodate the necessities of food creation with the safeguarding of biodiversity and biological system wellbeing. Agroforestry, cover trimming, and coordinated bother the board are among the practices that perceive the significance of plant variety in keeping up with soil richness, improving strength, and supporting valuable life forms. By adjusting farming practices to natural standards, it becomes conceivable to saddle the meaning of vegetation in supporting environments as well as the worldwide human populace.

Chapter 5

The Conductor's Baton - Environmental Factors

The director's rod is an integral asset, an apparently honest wand that holds the way to organizing an ensemble of sounds, forming the rhythmic movement of music. Nonetheless, past the domain of the show lobby, where the songs of life unfurl, there exists a more extensive orchestra — the natural factors that employ their impact over the director's mallet, influencing the music as well as the actual pith of presence.

Nature, with its unpredictable rhythms and harmonies, is a guide by its own doing. From the delicate stir of passes on in a timberland to the crashing crescendo of sea waves, the climate makes way for the stupendous presentation of life. In this complicated exchange, the guide's cudgel is directed not just by the hands of a human maestro yet by the concealed powers of environment, environment, and the fragile equilibrium of biological systems.

The ensemble of natural elements starts with the air we inhale — the undetectable guide that shapes the actual substance of our reality. The sythesis of the air, a sensitive mix of gases, organizes the environment, impacting weather conditions and deciding the destiny of biological systems. Ozone harming substances, similar to the notes in a score, add to the warming of the planet, assuming a part in the ensemble of environmental change.

As the cudgel climbs, the temperature of the World's surface answers with a unique scope of impacts. Ice covers dissolve, oceans rise, and weather conditions shift in a bedlam of climatic varieties. The natural elements, directed by the concealed hand of environmental change, work out in the rising force and recurrence of outrageous climate occasions — a violent development in the ensemble of the Anthropocene.

The stick stretches out its scope to the seas, where flows weave complex examples, conveying the beat of life. Maritime dissemination, driven by temperature and saltiness slopes, goes about as a quiet guide forming marine biological systems. Nonetheless, the persevering crescendo of human exercises, from overfishing to contamination, upsets the normal cadence of the oceans, making dissension in the once-amicable submerged ensemble.

Land, the earthly stage for the show of life, demonstrates the veracity of the effects of human exercises for a fantastic scope. Deforestation, the getting free from huge regions of backwoods, is likened to tearing pages from the melodic score of biodiversity. The guide's rod, rather than directing an amicable tune, witnesses the discord of territory misfortune, jeopardizing endless species and disintegrating the fragile equilibrium of biological systems.

In the unpredictable dance of life, biodiversity is the tune that resounds through biological systems. The director's twirly doo, directed by the hand of natural variables, assumes a critical part in coordinating the sensitive harmony between species. In any case, the dissonant notes of human exercises, like territory obliteration and the presentation of obtrusive species, upset this environmental concordance, prompting a deficiency of biodiversity at a disturbing rate.

The maestro's implement stretches out past the earthbound domain to the ethereal levels of the climate. The sythesis of air toxins, the noisy notes of industrialization, and the burning of non-renewable energy sources make a racket that resonates through the environment. As the implement rises, so does the centralization of contaminations, influencing air quality and human wellbeing in a conflicting ensemble of ecological corruption.

Water, a nurturing component, turns into a material whereupon the guide's rod paints its tune. However, the crescendo of water contamination, powered by modern overflow, rural synthetic compounds, and plastic waste, discolors this amphibian arrangement. The maestro's stick, when directing the progression of perfect waterways and lakes, presently fights with the strife of contaminated waters, compromising environments and the networks that rely upon them.

In the anthropogenic orchestra, the director's stick goes up against the mood of asset abuse. From the guts of the Earth, minerals and petroleum products are removed in a steady quest for monetary development. The once-musical scenes change into scars of extraction, abandoning ecological debasement and social cacophony. The maestro's rod, presently troubled with the heaviness of asset consumption, faces the test of organizing a reasonable future.

The musicality of human utilization reverberations through the guide's implement, forming the elements of waste age. From single-use plastics to electronic waste, the creation of present day life delivers a crescendo of disposed of materials. The maestro's cudgel, in this ensemble of waste, wrestles with the ecological results of an expendable culture, where the congruity of environments is muffled by the conflict of contamination.

The director's rod, when an image of imaginative articulation, turns into a representation for the decisions mankind makes in coordinating what's in store. The amicable orchestra of ecological variables, directed by the fragile equilibrium of nature, faces the danger of friction and cacophony. As the rod rises and falls, so too does the destiny of the planet, laced in the perplexing dance between human exercises and the sensitive biological systems that support life.

In this orchestra of ecological elements, the maestro's stick should be directed by another ethos — an ethos of supportability, protection, and an amicable concurrence with nature. The director's twirly doo turns into an encouraging sign, a device for coordinating a future where the sensitive equilibrium of biological systems is saved, and the tune of biodiversity keeps on resounding.

The ascent of natural mindfulness turns into a crescendo in the ensemble of progress. Protection endeavors, maintainable practices, and a worldwide obligation to address environmental change arise as the notes that can fit the harsh components of the anthropogenic ensemble. The guide's rod, when troubled by the heaviness of natural debasement, presently turns into an impetus for positive change.

Environmentally friendly power, another development in the ensemble, replaces the discordant harmonies of petroleum products. The director's implement, presently directed by the breezes and the sun, organizes a song of perfect, practical power. The concordance of this sustainable power orchestra resounds with the climate as well as with the commitment of a stronger and fair future.

Natural strategies, similar to the notes on a score, shape the heading of the orchestra. States and organizations, using the director's implement of regulation and guideline, assume a significant part in directing the symphony of human exercises towards supportability. The structure of regulations and strategies turns into the way to making an amicable harmony among improvement and natural stewardship.

Training arises as a crucial development in the orchestra of progress. The guide's rod, presently in the possession of educated and engaged people, directs a development towards ecological proficiency. A general public knowledgeable in the complexities of biological relationship turns into the ensemble that sings the gestures of recognition of protection and supportable living.

In the worldwide ensemble, joint effort turns into the fitting power. Countries, associations, and networks hold hands in an aggregate work to address ecological difficulties. The director's twirly doo, passed starting with one substance then onto the next, coordinates a worldwide development towards a practical future. Global participation turns into the song that rises above borders, cultivating a common obligation to the prosperity of the planet.

The guide's rod, when troubled by the dissonant notes of ecological corruption, presently ascends with restored reason. The orchestra of natural variables, led by a worldwide obligation to manageability, starts to resound with a tune of trust. The fragile equilibrium of environments, the cadence of biodiversity, and the concordance of a tough planet become the central places of this extraordinary organization.

As the director's twirly doo guides the ensemble towards an economical future, the story of natural stewardship becomes imbued in the social texture of social orders.

Workmanship, writing, and media become the expressive mediums through which the magnificence of nature and the desperation of ecological preservation are conveyed. The maestro's implement, presently an image of social edification, shapes the shared perspective towards an amicable concurrence with the Earth.

In the terrific finale of the natural ensemble, the guide's twirly doo takes a last bow. The crescendo of positive change reverberations through the scenes, seas, and skies. The sensitive equilibrium of biological systems, when near the precarious edge of discord, presently resonates with the versatile tune of a planet together as one.

The tradition of the guide's stick, in this last development, turns into a demonstration of the force of aggregate activity and the extraordinary capability of human organization. The ensemble of natural elements, when compromised by the friction of impractical practices, arises as a strong organization formed by the decisions and activities of humankind.

As the drapery falls on this ecological orchestra, another time starts — one where the director's rod stays an image of cautiousness, stewardship, and the getting through obligation to protect the magnificence and variety of our planet. The excursion towards manageability proceeds, directed by the agreeable transaction of natural elements and the immovable assurance of mankind to be the caretakers of a flourishing and strong Earth.

5.1 Explore the environmental factors that influence nature's symphony, such as climate, geography, and topography.

Nature's orchestra is an agreeable piece, a musical magnum opus led by the undetectable hand of ecological elements. As we investigate the unpredictable songs that resound through the normal world, we dig into the subtleties of environment, geology, and geography — the guides that shape the actual quintessence of nature's terrific presentation.

Environment, similar to the delicate maestro directing a melodic gathering, sets the overall state of mind for the orchestra of the Earth. It envelops the drawn out examples of temperature, moistness, wind, and precipitation, making the barometrical circumstances that characterize various districts. The director's implement of environment organizes the assorted biological systems we experience, from the bone chilling scenes of polar locales to the lavish woven artworks of tropical rainforests.

In the calm zones, where the stick moves with a delicate influence, deciduous woodlands answer with a yearly beat of variety evolving leaves. The evolving seasons, directed by the slant of the World's hub, direct the recurring pattern of life in these districts. Spring shows up as a crescendo, arousing lethargic widely varied vegetation, while fall denotes an elegant decrescendo, as nature plans for the hibernation of winter.

On the other hand, the director's rod of environment in bone-dry districts directs an orchestra of variation. Desert biological systems, with their strong verdure, have advanced to flourish despite shortage. The cudgel's unpretentious developments direct the planning of uncommon yet extreme precipitation, setting off an explosion of life in a generally cruel climate. Here, the orchestra is one of endurance, where plants and creatures dance to the musicality of inconsistent precipitation.

Moving to the tropical domains, the guide's twirly doo of environment takes on a more rich dance. The tropical locales, favored with bountiful daylight and warmth, encourage the development of rich rainforests. The ensemble of biodiversity arrives at its peak here, with a symphony of lively tones, various species, and a bedlam of sounds. However, this lavish tune isn't without its difficulties, as the implement's developments likewise achieve the danger of typhoons and the potential for natural interruption.

The geology of the Earth, much the same as the mind boggling game plan of melodic notes, assumes a crucial part in nature's orchestra. Mountains, valleys, fields, and levels — all add to the agreeable creation directed by the powers of nature. The rise coordinated by the guide's cudgel of geology establishes a powerful interaction that impacts environment, biological systems, and the dispersion of life.

High in the mountains, where the director's twirly doo ascends to grand levels, the orchestra takes on a snow capped song. Here, the air is flimsy, temperatures decrease, and life has adjusted to the difficulties of high heights. Glorious pinnacles become the stage for a remarkable group of greenery, tough even with outrageous circumstances. The ensemble of the mountains reverberations with the calls of slippery animals and the stir of strong vegetation.

Plunging to the marshes, where the cudgel clears across tremendous fields, the ensemble movements to the musicality of prairies and savannas. These open scenes, molded by the guide's cudgel of geography, support assorted environments where herbivores brush and hunters meander.

The dance of tall grasses in the breeze turns into a visual portrayal of the unobtrusive developments of the geographical mallet, making a powerful ensemble of life on the fields.

The guide's cudgel broadens its impact underneath the surface too. Seas, with their secret profundities and immense breadths, structure a necessary piece of nature's ensemble. The geography of the sea depths, molded by submerged mountains, channels, and fields, directs the progression of flows and the appropriation of marine life. The remote ocean ensemble, directed by the mallet of submerged geography, stays a strange and generally neglected organization.

Wetlands, with their novel mix of earthbound and oceanic qualities, likewise bear the engraving of the geological cudgel. The delicate undulations of the land make spaces for bogs and marshes, where the orchestra of creatures of land and water, bugs, and waterfowl unfurls. The geological guide shapes the hydrology of wetlands, impacting their job as regular channels and nurseries for a heap of animal categories.

In the fabulous coordination of nature, the cooperation among environment and geography turns into a vital development. The downpour shadow impact, a consequence of mountains blocking sodden air masses, makes a glaring difference among windward and leeward sides. The guide's stick, rising and falling with the geology, directs the dissemination of precipitation, bringing about rich timberlands on one side and bone-dry scenes on the other.

Nature's orchestra isn't just led by the great developments of environment and geography yet additionally by the unpretentious varieties in soil sythesis. The edaphic factors, directed by the director's rod of geography, assume a part in molding the ensemble of vegetation. From the supplement rich soils of stream valleys to the supplement unfortunate soils of rough outcrops, the land cudgel organizes the circumstances that help different biological systems.

The land director's mallet stretches out its impact to the arrangement of caverns, gullies, and other geographical elements that become one of a kind stages in nature's orchestra. In cave biological systems, where haziness wins, particular life forms have advanced to flourish without a trace of light. The topographical mallet shapes these secret domains, making territories that are both puzzling and delicate.

Streams, directed by the geographical implement and formed by topographical powers, cut their direction through the scene, making dynamic environments along their banks. The progression of water, impacted by the guide's mallet of geography, shapes valleys and supports a rich embroidery of life. Riparian natural surroundings, where land meets water, become indispensable passages for biodiversity, making an ensemble that blends the components of both earthbound and sea-going environments.

As we investigate the ecological elements forming nature's orchestra, the complex dance of biodiversity turns into a point of convergence. The guide's cudgel of environmental collaborations, where species coincide and rely upon each other, assumes a urgent part in keeping up with the sensitive equilibrium of biological systems. The orchestra of hunter prey connections, mutualistic organizations, and the snare of life makes a unique piece that mirrors the interconnectedness of every living thing.

Relocation, directed by the undetectable hand of ecological elements, turns into a development in the ensemble of life. Birds, well evolved creatures, and even bugs set out on incredible excursions, following the stick of occasional changes, temperature varieties, and asset accessibility. The ensemble of movement traverses landmasses, as species navigate immense distances looking for reasonable territories, molding the biodiversity of various districts.

Fire, a basic power in nature, likewise assumes a part in the orchestra led by ecological variables. The cudgel of environmental fire, molded by environment, geology, and vegetation, impacts the design and sythesis of biological systems. In fire-adjusted scenes, for example, savannas and specific kinds of timberlands, the guide's rod directs the recurrence and power of flames, making environments that rely upon occasional consuming for recovery.

Human exercises, nonetheless, bring cacophony into nature's orchestra. The guide's twirly doo, when directed by the hand of natural equilibrium, presently fights with the disagreement of deforestation, contamination, and environmental change.

The anthropogenic development in the ensemble compromises biodiversity, upsets environments, and modifies the actual arrangement of the normal world.

The investigation of ecological variables forming nature's orchestra carries us to the front of preservation and natural stewardship. The guide's twirly doo, when held exclusively by the powers of nature, presently calls for human intercession to reestablish congruity. Preservation endeavors, directed by a comprehension of the complex connections between environment, geology, geography, and biodiversity, become the notes that can achieve a positive change in the ensemble of the Earth.

Safeguarded regions, laid out fully intent on saving the variety of life, become safe-havens where the guide's rod can move openly. Public parks, marine stores, and untamed life asylums address purposeful endeavors to defend the ensemble of nature from the disharmony of human effect. The twirly doo of preservation organizes a song of trust, where environments can recuperate and biodiversity can flourish.

In the worldwide development towards maintainability, the director's mallet reaches out to arrangements and practices that perceive the worth of nature's orchestra.

Maintainable land the executives, dependable asset extraction, and the change to sustainable power sources become essential developments in the ensemble of natural protection. The rod of manageability expects to blend human exercises with the regular world, guaranteeing a versatile and adjusted planet.

Schooling turns into a strong development in the ensemble, as the guide's cudgel of information and mindfulness guides social orders towards a more profound comprehension of the climate. Ecological proficiency, combined with an appreciation for the complexities of nature's ensemble, turns into the way to encouraging a feeling of obligation and stewardship. The cudgel of instruction shapes an age that is receptive to the necessities of the planet, fit for directing an agreeable relationship with the Earth.

In the fabulous finale of nature's ensemble, the guide's cudgel ascends to a crescendo — a call for worldwide cooperation. Global participation turns into the critical development in the ensemble of ecological protection. Countries join together, perceiving that the difficulties looked by one are difficulties looked by all.

5.2 Discuss the delicate balance and the impact of human activities on the environment.

The sensitive equilibrium of the climate is a perplexing and multifaceted ensemble, where the different parts of the regular world orchestrate to make a supportable and versatile planet. In any case, as mankind has developed and extended, our exercises have progressively upset this sensitive harmony, bringing conflict into nature's ensemble. The effect of human exercises on the climate is significant, enveloping a large number of elements that influence environments, biodiversity, environment, and the general soundness of the planet.

One of the essential manners by which human exercises upset the fragile equilibrium of the climate is through environment obliteration. As populaces develop and urbanization extends, normal natural surroundings are cleared for horticulture, framework advancement, and human settlements. This adjustment of scenes uproots innumerable species as well as sections environments, making it trying for untamed life to track down reasonable living spaces and disturbing biological cycles.

Deforestation, a huge driver of territory obliteration, has expansive results. The getting free from huge plots of woods for lumber, horticulture, and different purposes eliminates imperative carbon sinks as well as adds to the deficiency of biodiversity. Timberlands, frequently alluded to as the lungs of the Earth, assume a pivotal part in managing the worldwide environment by retaining carbon dioxide during photosynthesis. The interruption of this normal cycle enhances the effects of environmental change.

Besides, the fragile equilibrium is additionally tipped by the presentation of obtrusive species. Human exercises, like worldwide exchange and travel, have worked with the development of species past their regular environments. Intrusive species can outcompete local widely varied vegetation, disturb food networks, and even lead to the annihilation of local species. The obtrusive species become a noisy note in the orchestra of environments, frequently making irreversible harm neighborhood biodiversity.

The extraction of normal assets, one more key human action, has significant ramifications for the climate. Mining, for instance, includes the expulsion of a lot of earth, modifying scenes and frequently abandoning scars of ecological debasement. The extraction of petroleum derivatives adds to air and water contamination, and the burning of these powers discharges ozone harming substances, heightening the worldwide environment emergency.

Water assets are likewise altogether impacted by human exercises. The release of toxins into waterways and lakes, whether from modern cycles or rural overflow, taints freshwater biological systems. Over-extraction of water for horticulture, industry, and homegrown use can prompt the exhaustion of springs and the evaporating of streams, influencing both earthly and sea-going environments.

The effect of human exercises on the climate stretches out to the environment, where air contamination has turned into an inescapable issue. Modern discharges, vehicle exhaust, and the copying of petroleum derivatives discharge toxins like particulate matter, nitrogen oxides, and sulfur dioxide out of sight. These contaminations hurt human wellbeing as well as add to exhaust cloud arrangement, corrosive downpour, and the decay of air quality, affecting environments and untamed life.

Maybe the most squeezing and universally perceived effect of human exercises on the climate will be environmental change. The consuming of non-renewable energy sources, deforestation, and modern cycles discharge ozone harming substances — essentially carbon dioxide — into the climate. These gases trap heat, prompting a warming of the World's surface and disturbance of long-laid out environment designs. The outcomes are expansive, including more continuous and serious heatwaves, changing precipitation designs, rising ocean levels, and an expansion in the recurrence and power of outrageous climate occasions.

The sensitive equilibrium of the climate is unpredictably attached to environment soundness. Environments have developed over centuries to adjust to explicit climatic circumstances, and any huge deviation from these circumstances can have flowing impacts. As human-prompted environmental change speeds up, biological systems battle to adjust, prompting disturbances in the planning of occasional occasions, changes in species circulations, and, at times, the breakdown of whole biological systems.

The effect of human exercises on the climate isn't restricted to the actual domain. Overexploitation of regular assets, driven by monetary interests, has prompted the exhaustion of fisheries, loss of biodiversity, and the debasement of biological systems. Impractical rural works on, including the utilization of synthetic composts and pesticides, add to soil debasement and water contamination, compromising the capacity of biological systems to help life.

The sensitive equilibrium of the climate is additionally affected by the amazing measure of waste produced by human social orders. From plastic contamination in seas to electronic waste filling landfills, the results of our expendable culture are significant. Inappropriate garbage removal hurts untamed life and biological systems as well as postures dangers to human wellbeing, as poisons from disposed of items can filter into the climate.

The deficiency of biodiversity, an immediate consequence of human exercises, is a basic part of the ecological emergency. Species annihilation rates are speeding up, and whole biological systems are unwinding. The sensitive exchange between species, where each assumes an extraordinary part in keeping up with natural equilibrium, is disturbed when key species are lost. Biodiversity misfortune lessens the versatility of environments as well as decreases the accessibility of fundamental biological system administrations whereupon human social orders depend.

The effect of human exercises on the climate isn't uniform; it excessively influences weak networks and worsens social imbalances. Ecological corruption frequently hits underestimated populaces the hardest, as they will generally depend all the more straightforwardly on regular assets for their vocations. The deficiency of arable land, admittance to clean water, and openness to ecological risks excessively influence those with restricted assets and political power.

Tending to the effect of human exercises on the climate requires a far reaching and foundational approach. Preservation endeavors assume a vital part in saving biodiversity and safeguarding environments. Laying out and overseeing safeguarded regions, executing maintainable land-use rehearses, and reestablishing corrupted natural surroundings are fundamental techniques to relieve the harm brought about by environment annihilation and biodiversity misfortune.

Reasonable asset the board is vital in guaranteeing that the extraction of normal assets doesn't prompt irreversible natural corruption. Practices like feasible ranger service, dependable mining, and fisheries the executives expect to offset human necessities with the conservation of biological systems. The reception of roundabout economy standards, which underline decreasing, reusing, and reusing materials, is likewise a critical technique to limit the ecological effect of asset extraction and waste age.

Progressing to sustainable power sources is an essential move toward moderating the effect of human exercises on the climate, especially in tending to environmental change. Sun powered, wind, hydroelectric, and other environmentally friendly power innovations offer cleaner options in contrast to petroleum derivatives, decreasing ozone depleting substance outflows and relieving the warming of the planet. Interest in environmentally friendly power framework and the eliminating of petroleum derivative endowments are basic parts of a feasible energy progress.

Endeavors to check air and water contamination require severe guidelines and the reception of cleaner advancements. Modern discharges can be diminished through the execution of contamination control measures and the change to cleaner creation processes. Essentially, implementing guidelines on vehicle outflows, advancing public transportation, and putting resources into supportable metropolitan arranging can add to further developing air quality in metropolitan regions.

Water protection and economical water the executives rehearses are vital for defend freshwater biological systems and guarantee a steady stockpile of clean water for both human networks and the climate. Executing measures to decrease contamination, safeguarding watersheds, and advancing productive water use in farming and industry are basic parts of maintainable water the executives.

Relieving the effect of human exercises on the climate likewise includes encouraging a change in shopper conduct and advancing practical ways of life. Instructing general society about the natural results of utilization decisions, empowering mindful waste administration, and supporting eco-accommodating items and administrations add to lessening the by and large biological impression of human social orders.

Worldwide participation is principal in tending to worldwide natural difficulties. Environmental change, biodiversity misfortune, and contamination are transboundary issues that require cooperative endeavors on a worldwide scale. Arrangements, for example, the Paris Settlement on environmental change and the Show on Organic Variety embody worldwide endeavors to altogether handle these difficulties. Maintaining and reinforcing these arrangements, alongside cultivating worldwide fortitude, are essential moves toward exploring a feasible future.

Ecological equity is a basic part of tending to the effect of human exercises on the climate. Perceiving and correcting verifiable and current natural treacheries is fundamental for building an additional evenhanded and maintainable world. This includes guaranteeing that underestimated networks have a voice in ecological dynamic cycles, approach natural advantages, and are safeguarded from unbalanced ecological weights.

5.3 Emphasize the need for sustainable practices to preserve the symphony.

The dire call for maintainable practices reverberates as a focal topic in the worldwide story on ecological protection. As mankind remains at the crossing point of natural emergencies and extraordinary ecological corruption, the basic to take on economical practices turns out to be progressively apparent. This basic is established in the acknowledgment that the sensitive equilibrium of the regular world, similar to an orchestra, requires an agreeable joint effort between human exercises and the planet's environments. The requirement for manageable practices isn't only an idea yet a major essential for protecting the orchestra of nature.

Supportability, at its center, involves addressing the necessities of the present without compromising the capacity of people in the future to address their own issues. It is a call for balance, for a cognizant and capable way to deal with asset usage that thinks about the drawn out soundness of the climate. At the core of manageable practices lies a significant comprehension of the interconnectedness of biological, social, and financial frameworks.

The ensemble of nature, with its mind boggling tunes of biodiversity, environment strength, and energetic biological systems, is under danger from a crescendo of unreasonable practices. Boss among these is the dependence on petroleum products for energy, a noisy note that resonates through the environment as ozone depleting substance emanations. The consuming of coal, oil, and petroleum gas adds to air contamination as well as increases the warming of the planet, disturbing the painstakingly arranged environment designs that biological systems rely upon.

Changing to environmentally friendly power sources stands apart as a critical development in the ensemble of manageability. Sun oriented, wind, hydropower, and other clean energy innovations offer an agreeable option in contrast to the conflicting murmur of petroleum derivatives. The director's cudgel, presently directed by the breezes and the sun, organizes a song that mitigates environmental change, diminishes air contamination, and decreases the natural impression of energy creation. Putting resources into sustainable power foundation and getting rid of petroleum product sponsorships become instrumental in this groundbreaking development.

Supportable agribusiness is another key development that reverberates inside the orchestra of ecological protection. Customary farming practices, set apart by the weighty utilization of substance manures, pesticides, and monoculture, frequently upset the regular equilibrium of biological systems. Soil debasement, loss of biodiversity, and water contamination are the discordant reverberations of unreasonable cultivating strategies. The requirement for a shift towards regenerative horticulture becomes fundamental — a training that underscores soil wellbeing, biodiversity, and natural strength.

In the orchestra of economical horticulture, agroecology arises as an agreeable development. This approach coordinates biological standards into horticultural frameworks, advancing biodiversity, improving soil ripeness, and limiting the utilization of outer information sources. Agroforestry, cover editing, and trim pivot become the notes that make a tune out of flexibility, where the soundness of the land is entwined with the prosperity of networks. Neighborhood and native information, profoundly receptive to the rhythms of nature, assumes a critical part in directing manageable rural practices.

The preservation of biodiversity, a foundation of natural manageability, requires intentional and purposeful endeavors. The fragile transaction of species, where each satisfies an extraordinary job in keeping up with environmental equilibrium, is under danger from territory obliteration, contamination, and environmental change. Safeguarded regions, decisively assigned to shield basic environments, become the asylums that permit the orchestra of biodiversity to flourish. Practical land-use arranging, natural surroundings reclamation, and the foundation of biological halls interface these safeguarded regions, permitting species to move openly and guaranteeing the versatility of environments.

Manageable ranger service rehearses arise as a critical development in the ensemble of biodiversity preservation. The aimless logging of backwoods, frequently determined by momentary monetary interests, disturbs the living space of endless species and adds to deforestation. The reception of economical ranger service standards, like specific logging, reforestation, and local area based timberland the executives, turns into a tune that reverberations through the forested scenes. Accreditation programs like the Timberland Stewardship Gathering (FSC) guarantee that wood and wood items come from reasonably oversaw backwoods, advancing dependable stewardship of this basic asset.

Marine environments, indispensable parts of the worldwide ensemble, face horde dangers from overfishing, natural surroundings obliteration, and contamination. Impractical fishing rehearses, portrayed by overharvesting and bycatch, drain fish stocks and upset marine food networks. Embracing maintainable fisheries the board turns into the directing development in the marine protection orchestra. Science-based shares, marine safeguarded regions, and the advancement of mindful fishing rehearses add to the rebuilding and protection of marine biological systems.

Plastic contamination, a grating note in the ensemble of seas, has arrived at disturbing levels. Single-use plastics, bundling materials, and disposed of waste add to the debasement of marine conditions, hurting marine life and biological systems. The requirement for feasible waste administration rehearses turns into a reverberating development in the ensemble of sea protection. Reusing, decrease of plastic use, and the improvement of elective materials add to a song that looks to reestablish the strength of marine environments.

The round economy arises as an extraordinary development in the ensemble of supportability. Rather than the direct model of take, make, and arrange, the roundabout economy imagines a regenerative framework where assets are saved being used as far as might be feasible, with insignificant waste age. Reusing, upcycling, and reusing materials become necessary notes in this tune of supportability. The round economy expects to break liberated from the straight requirements of asset exhaustion and ecological debasement, introducing an agreeable way to deal with creation and utilization.

Manageable metropolitan arranging turns into a vital development in the ensemble of ecological preservation. Quick urbanization, frequently described by rambling turn of events, gridlock, and insufficient green spaces, presents critical difficulties to the fragile equilibrium of environments. Reasonable urban areas, planned with standards of walkability, green foundation, and energy productivity, become the ensemble's tribute to versatile and bearable metropolitan conditions. Metropolitan arranging that focuses on open transportation, green rooftops, and sustainable power reconciliation adds to the agreeable concurrence of human social orders and the climate.

Water preservation and maintainable water the board structure a fundamental development in the orchestra of ecological supportability. Freshwater assets, fundamental for biological systems, agribusiness, and human networks, are under expanding strain from over-extraction, contamination, and environmental change. Reasonable water rehearses underscore productive water use, contamination avoidance, and the insurance of watersheds. Executing water-saving innovations, reestablishing wetlands, and advancing capable water utilization add to the song of water maintainability.

Schooling and mindfulness become instrumental developments in the ensemble of supportability. Natural proficiency, established in a comprehension of environmental standards, encourages a feeling of obligation and stewardship. Instruction about the effects of human exercises on the climate, the worth of biodiversity, and the significance of supportable practices turns into the guide's implement, directing social orders towards a more agreeable relationship with the planet.

The confidential area, as a central member in the worldwide economy, holds the ability to shape the ensemble of supportability. Corporate maintainability rehearses, directed by standards of natural obligation, social value, and monetary reasonability, become extraordinary developments. Organizations taking on supportable inventory network works on, diminishing their carbon impression, and focusing on natural and social administration add to a tune that adjusts monetary exercises to the prosperity of the planet.

Government approaches and guidelines arise as vital developments in the ensemble of supportability. Upholding natural guidelines, boosting manageable practices, and cultivating development through strategy support add to an amicable system for maintainability.

The foundation of aggressive outflow decrease focuses on, the advancement of environmentally friendly power, and the joining of maintainability into public improvement plans become notes in the tune of administration for a practical future.

Worldwide participation, urgent for tending to worldwide natural difficulties, turns into the all-encompassing development in the orchestra of maintainability. Environmental change, biodiversity misfortune, and contamination are transboundary issues that require cooperative endeavors on a worldwide scale. Arrangements, for example, the Paris Understanding and the Show on Organic Variety embody global responsibilities to on the whole handle these difficulties. Maintaining and reinforcing these arrangements, alongside cultivating worldwide fortitude, become the orchestra's song of praise for a reasonable and versatile world.

Safeguarding the orchestra of nature has turned into a basic even with heightening ecological difficulties. The fragile equilibrium that organizes the interconnectedness of biological systems, biodiversity, and the environment is under consistent danger from human exercises. Perceiving this, the need to safeguard the ensemble has arisen as a mobilizing require a more agreeable conjunction among mankind and the planet. In this critical journey, a multi-layered approach is required, enveloping preservation endeavors, supportable practices, and a significant change in cultural perspectives toward the climate.

Saving biodiversity stands apart as an essential development in the orchestra of conservation. Biodiversity, the assortment of life on The planet, is fundamental for the flexibility and versatility of biological systems. The many-sided transaction of species in their normal territories makes an ensemble of natural equilibrium, where every creature assumes a novel part. Be that as it may, uncontrolled natural surroundings obliteration, contamination, and environmental change have encouraged a biodiversity emergency, with species confronting elimination at an extraordinary rate.

Safeguarded regions, assigned to save basic territories and biodiversity areas of interest, arise as safe-havens in the ensemble of protection. Public parks, untamed life stores, and marine safeguarded regions become stages where the ensemble of nature can unfurl without the cacophony of human impedance. Successful administration and requirement of these safeguarded regions are vital, guaranteeing that the sensitive equilibrium inside these biological systems stays in salvageable shape.

Reasonable ranger service rehearses become instrumental notes in the orchestra of preservation. Woodlands, frequently alluded to as the lungs of the Earth, are crucial for carbon sequestration, environment guideline, and natural surroundings protection. Unreasonable logging, driven by financial interests, has prompted deforestation and the deficiency of endless species.

Embracing economical ranger service rehearses, like specific logging and reforestation, guarantees that the ensemble of the backwoods perseveres, offering environmental types of assistance and keeping up with biodiversity.

Marine protection, fundamental for the safeguarding of the orchestra, addresses the difficulties looked by seas and their occupants. Overfishing, environment annihilation, and plastic contamination undermine marine biological systems, disturbing the fragile equilibrium of submerged life. Laying out marine safeguarded regions, managing fishing rehearses, and handling plastic waste add to the reclamation and conservation of the ensemble of the oceans. Feasible fisheries the executives turns into a directing development, guaranteeing that fish stocks can renew, supporting the livelihoods of waterfront networks and keeping up with the respectability of marine environments.

The orchestra of safeguarding reaches out to the reception of manageable farming practices. Horticulture, a key human movement, can possibly either blend with nature or disturb the sensitive equilibrium. Customary cultivating, set apart by escalated synthetic use and monoculture, frequently prompts soil corruption, biodiversity misfortune, and water contamination. Maintainable horticulture, established in agro-ecological standards, underscores soil wellbeing, biodiversity protection, and environmental versatility.

Regenerative horticulture arises as a groundbreaking development in the orchestra of practical cultivating. This approach centers around reestablishing and upgrading soil wellbeing, sequestering carbon, and advancing biodiversity. Cover editing, crop turn, and agroforestry become vital notes in regenerative horticulture, making a song of versatility where the soundness of the land is entwined with the prosperity of networks. Nearby and native information, profoundly associated with the rhythms of nature, assumes a significant part in directing feasible farming practices.

The safeguarding of freshwater biological systems turns into a fundamental development in the orchestra of protection. Streams, lakes, and wetlands are basic parts of the worldwide water cycle, supporting different oceanic life and offering fundamental types of assistance for human social orders. Notwithstanding, water contamination, over-extraction, and environment annihilation present critical dangers to freshwater biodiversity. Feasible water the board works on, including the security of watersheds, proficient water use, and contamination avoidance, add to the conservation of the ensemble of freshwater biological systems.

Tending to environmental change turns into an overall development in the ensemble of conservation. The consuming of petroleum derivatives, deforestation, and modern exercises discharge ozone depleting substances into the environment, prompting an Earth-wide temperature boost and environment unsteadiness.

The outcomes of environmental change, from more regular and serious heatwaves to rising ocean levels, present existential dangers to biological systems and human social orders the same. Relieving environmental change requires a coordinated work to lessen ozone harming substance outflows, progress to sustainable power sources, and adjust to the evolving environment.

Sustainable power, as an extraordinary development, assumes a vital part in the ensemble of environment activity. Sun based, wind, hydropower, and other clean energy advancements offer economical options in contrast to petroleum products. The director's twirly doo, presently directed by the breezes and the sun, coordinates a tune that mitigates environmental change, diminishes air contamination, and reduces the natural impression of energy creation. Interest in sustainable power framework and the eliminating of non-renewable energy source endowments become instrumental in this groundbreaking development.

The roundabout economy arises as an amicable development in the ensemble of maintainability. As opposed to the direct model of take, make, and arrange, the roundabout economy imagines a regenerative framework where assets are saved being used to the extent that this would be possible, with negligible waste age. Reusing, upcycling, and reusing materials become basic notes in this tune of maintainability. The round economy plans to break liberated from the straight imperatives of asset exhaustion and natural debasement, introducing an amicable way to deal with creation and utilization.

Maintainable metropolitan arranging turns into a critical development in the orchestra of ecological protection. Quick urbanization, frequently portrayed by rambling turn of events, gridlock, and deficient green spaces, presents huge difficulties to the fragile equilibrium of biological systems. Feasible urban communities, planned with standards of walkability, green framework, and energy effectiveness, become the orchestra's tribute to strong and reasonable metropolitan conditions. Metropolitan arranging that focuses on open transportation, green rooftops, and sustainable power reconciliation adds to the agreeable concurrence of human social orders and the climate.

Protecting the ensemble requires a significant change in cultural perspectives and ways of behaving toward the climate. Training and mindfulness become instrumental developments in this change. Natural education, established in a comprehension of biological standards, encourages a feeling of obligation and stewardship. Schooling about the effects of human exercises on the climate, the worth of biodiversity, and the significance of feasible practices turns into the guide's rod, directing social orders toward a more agreeable relationship with the planet.

The confidential area, as a central member in the worldwide economy, holds the ability to shape the orchestra of protection.

Corporate supportability rehearses, directed by standards of ecological obligation, social value, and financial practicality, become groundbreaking developments. Organizations taking on feasible inventory network works on, decreasing their carbon impression, and focusing on natural and social administration add to a tune that adjusts financial exercises to the prosperity of the planet.

Government approaches and guidelines arise as crucial developments in the orchestra of supportability. Upholding ecological guidelines, boosting feasible practices, and cultivating development through strategy support add to an amicable system for maintainability. The foundation of aggressive emanation decrease focuses on, the advancement of environmentally friendly power, and the reconciliation of supportability into public improvement plans become notes in the tune of administration for a maintainable future.

Worldwide collaboration, essential for tending to worldwide natural difficulties, turns into the overall development in the orchestra of conservation. Environmental change, biodiversity misfortune, and contamination are transboundary issues that require cooperative endeavors on a worldwide scale. Arrangements, for example, the Paris Understanding and the Show on Organic Variety embody global responsibilities to all in all handle these difficulties. Maintaining and reinforcing these arrangements, alongside cultivating worldwide fortitude, become the orchestra's hymn for a manageable and strong world.

Chapter 6

The Harmony of Water

In the ensemble of presence, water assumes a significant and pervasive part, winding around its fluid ringlets through the embroidery of life. The Congruity of Water is a story that investigates the diverse idea of water, digging into its basic quintessence, its extraordinary power, and its many-sided hit the dance floor with the world it maintains. From the littlest beads to the tremendous seas, water's presence is both unpretentious and fantastic, a quiet power molding the actual texture of our planet.

At its center, water is a particle, a straightforward association of two hydrogen molecules and one oxygen iota. However, this apparently honest mix has phenomenal properties that make it a foundation of life as far as we might be concerned. Its novel capacity to exist in three states — strong, fluid, and gas — highlights its flexibility and versatility. This smoothness isn't simply physical however stretches out to its job in environments, atmospheric conditions, and the unpredictable equilibrium of the regular world.

The excursion of water starts high above, where it appears as vaporous mists that float across the sky. The sensitive dance of buildup and vanishing is organized by the sun, a heavenly maestro whose beams give the energy expected to these natural changes. The mists, pregnant with dampness, set out on a divine excursion, directed by the impulses of the breeze. This elevated expressive dance finishes in the arrival of fluid gems upon the earth — a delicate downpour that sustains the dirt and extinguishes the thirst of vegetation the same.

As raindrops plunge, they start a cadenced outpouring, a percussion segment in the ensemble of water. Every drop carries with it the commitment of life, a remedy that renews streams, lakes, and springs. These waterways, similar to veins flowing through the earth, structure the circulatory arrangement of our planet. They shape scenes, cut gulches, and give living spaces to an astounding exhibit of life forms.

Streams, specifically, are the courses that convey the soul of landmasses. They wander through valleys, slicing through rock and soil, chiseling the landscape with a patient and tenacious elegance. The Nile, the Amazon, the Ganges — these famous waterways are not simple conduits; they are narrators, portraying the historical backdrop of civic establishments that have prospered along their banks. Their waters have seen the ascent and fall of realms, the introduction of societies, and the progression of time itself.

However, water's impact stretches out past the earthly domain. Seas, covering more than 66% of the World's surface, are the huge supplies of life. Underneath their surface lies a universe of marvels, an environment overflowing with animals of every kind. Coral reefs, the rainforests of the ocean, harbor a kaleidoscope of marine life, from the energetic shades of exotic fish to the lofty developments of effortless whales. The sea, with its musical tides and secretive profundities, stays a wellspring of motivation and wonderment, helping us to remember the unlimited secrets that stay underneath the surface.

Water, in any case, isn't simply a detached background to the show of life; it is a functioning member, forming and chiseling the very scenes it crosses. Disintegration, a quiet craftsman, cuts mind boggling designs into rock developments, changing mountains into valleys and shores into masterpieces. The Fabulous Gulch, a demonstration of the erosive force of water over ages, remains as a magnificent demonstration of the patient hand of time.

In the core of this watery ensemble, the idea of equilibrium arises as a focal topic. The fragile balance among precipitation and vanishing, among inflow and outpouring, characterizes the wellbeing of biological systems. Human exercises, in any case, have disturbed this normal congruity. Deforestation, urbanization, and environmental change have modified the elements of the water cycle, prompting dry spells, floods, and a large group of biological difficulties.

As we explore the complicated connection among mankind and water, it becomes apparent that our activities hold the way to reestablishing or further disturbing this fragile harmony. The journey for feasible water the executives isn't simply an ecological basic however a cultural obligation. Preservation endeavors, mechanical developments, and strategy mediations are fundamental parts of an agreeable future where water is loved and secured.

In the parched scenes that endure the worst part of water shortage, the worth of each and every drop turns out to be intensely obvious. From antiquated civilizations that excelled at water system to current cultures wrestling with water pressure, the significance of water preservation rises above time and boundaries. Developments in water-effective horticulture, wastewater reusing, and desalination advances offer looks at a future where water shortage is moderated through human creativity.

The Agreement of Water stretches out past the earthly domain, venturing into the tiny area where the substance of life itself is molded. Inside the bounds of living cells, water isn't simply a dissolvable; it is the medium through which biochemical responses unfurl. The dance of atoms in fluid conditions coordinates the complicated expressive dance of life, from the replication of DNA to the blend of proteins that structure the structure blocks of living creatures.

In the human body, water is the quiet guide of crucial cycles. It manages temperature, works with supplement transport, and gives a greasing up pad to joints. The human mind, washed in cerebrospinal liquid, depends on water for electrical conductivity and effective brain correspondence. The complicated transaction among hydration and wellbeing highlights the private association between our bodies and the essential pith of water.

The excursion of water through the human experience isn't simply physiological; it is profoundly social and otherworldly. Across developments and across time, water has been an image of cleansing, recharging, and greatness. Customs of submersion, representative inundations, and consecrated wells bear demonstration of the emblematic power attributed to water in the human mind. Its purging touch isn't simply physical yet profound, a course for the restoration of the spirit.

In writing and workmanship, water arises as a strong illustration, mirroring the back and forth movement of human feelings and the unyielding section of time. The verse of water is woven into the refrains of antiquated texts and the materials of magnum opuses. From the despairing profundities of a blustery day to the tempestuous floods of turbulent oceans, water fills in as a mirror to the human experience, an impression of our delights, distresses, and the transient idea of presence.

The investigation of water's concordance stretches out to the domain of sound, where the delicate stream of a stream, the musical accident of sea waves, and the loud thunder of cascades make a characteristic ensemble. The hear-able charm of water rises above social limits, reverberating with a general harmony that addresses the base association among humankind and the natural world. The hypnotizing hints of water summon a feeling of serenity, a sonic ointment that relieves the spirit and encourages a significant feeling of association with nature.

However, the agreement of water isn't immune. The apparition of contamination looms over the immaculateness of water, compromising biological systems, human wellbeing, and the sensitive equilibrium of sea-going conditions. Modern releases, horticultural overflow, and plastic waste blemish the clearness of once-flawless waters, changing them into dim impressions of human effect. The criticalness of tending to water contamination isn't simply an ecological basic yet an ethical obligation to shield the honesty of the environments that support life.

Notwithstanding these difficulties, the basic to safeguard water assets turns into a revitalizing call for aggregate activity. Promotion for clean water, feasible practices, and ecological stewardship becomes the dominant focal point in the worldwide discussion on preservation. The affirmation that admittance to clean water is a major basic liberty highlights the moral components of water the board, underlining the requirement for fair conveyance and mindful utilization.

In the complex dance of water, environmental change arises as a strong disruptor, modifying precipitation designs, strengthening outrageous climate occasions, and reshaping the topography of water accessibility. Rising ocean levels infringe upon seaside territories, compromising both human networks and biodiversity. The basic to address environmental change and its effect on water assets turns into a foundation of a versatile and reasonable future.

The account of water isn't bound to the earthbound domain; it stretches out its span to the universe. The investigation of heavenly bodies uncovers hints of water as ice on far off planets and moons. The quest for extraterrestrial life depends on the presence of water, a widespread dissolvable that gives the fundamental circumstances to the science of life to unfurl. The tempting possibility of finding water past Earth starts the creative mind and highlights the interconnectedness of the universe.

As we explore the complex embroidery of The Concordance of Water, we are defied with a significant truth — the destiny of water is indistinguishable from the predetermination of mankind. Our decisions, exclusively and on the whole, reverberation through the watersheds of time, molding the heritage we leave for people in the future. The basic to love, secure, and support water assets isn't simply an ecological reason however a demonstration of our common obligation as stewards of the planet we call home.

In the end notes of this investigation, The Concordance of Water arises as an immortal song that reverberates across the ages of human life. From the early stage seas that supported the starting points of life to the cutting edge difficulties of preservation and environmental change, water winds around a story that rises above the limits of existence.

6.1 Investigate the role of water bodies in shaping the symphony of nature.

In the great embroidery of nature, water bodies arise as key orchestrators, molding an ensemble that reverberates through environments, scenes, and the perplexing snare of life. This examination dives into the multi-layered job of water bodies in this ensemble, investigating their extraordinary impact on the climate, their essential commitments to biodiversity, and the many-sided exchange among water and the different components of the regular world.

Water bodies, going from quiet lakes to strong streams and sweeping seas, are dynamic substances that assume a vital part in forming the physical and environmental qualities of the locales they cross. Their impact starts with the basic hydrological cycle, a never-ending dance that includes the vanishing of water from surfaces, its excursion through the climate, and its inevitable re-visitation of Earth as precipitation. This cycle is the heartbeat of the ensemble, a musical stream that supports life and shapes scenes.

One of the essential ways water bodies shape the climate is through the course of disintegration. Waterways, with their interminable stream, step by step erode rock and soil, cutting valleys and forming the geography of the land. The famous Stupendous Gulch remains as a demonstration of the erosive force of water after some time, a superb demonstration of the patient chiseling of the World's surface by streaming water. Past making geographical marvels, this cycle impacts soil ripeness, supplement transport, and the appropriation of dregs, shaping the establishment for different environments.

Lakes, with their serene surfaces and intelligent profundities, act as repositories of life and reflections of the encompassing scene. They are not simple waterways; they are dynamic biological systems that help a rich embroidery of vegetation. Wetlands, frequently found at the edges of lakes and waterways, are biodiversity areas of interest that give fundamental environment to various species. From transitory birds to oceanic plants, these biological systems flourish in the sensitive equilibrium of water accessibility, making a mosaic of life that adds to the general biodiversity of the district.

The ensemble of nature stretches out to the seas, immense spans that cover more than 66% of the World's surface. Seas, with their cadenced tides and strange profundities, house a mind boggling cluster of marine life. Coral reefs, frequently alluded to as the rainforests of the ocean, are lively biological systems that abound with biodiversity. The unpredictable dance of water flows, temperature varieties, and supplement cycles in the seas makes territories for a different scope of animal groups, from minute tiny fish to lofty whales.

Inside water bodies, the interaction among amphibian and earthbound biological systems makes momentary zones known as riparian regions. These zones, tracked down along the banks of streams and lakes, act as vital territories and conductors for biodiversity. Riparian vegetation, adjusted to both wet and dry circumstances, balances out banks, channels contaminations, and gives conceal. These regions are imperative for the endurance of numerous species, going about as passageways that empower development and movement across scenes.

The connection between water bodies and biodiversity is many-sided and co-operative. The accessibility and nature of water straightforwardly impact the kinds of species that can flourish in a specific climate. Freshwater environments, for example, streams and lakes, support an extraordinary arrangement of creatures adjusted to life in streaming or standing water. Fish species, for instance, display different transformations to the particular states of their sea-going natural surroundings, from quick streaming streams to in any case lakes.

The interconnectedness of water bodies turns out to be much more clear while considering the relocation examples of numerous species. Waterways, going about as normal parkways, work with the development of fish, creatures of land and water, and other amphibian organic entities. The yearly movement of salmon, exploring waterways to generate in their natal streams, is a demonstration of the job of water bodies as channels for life cycles. Likewise, wetlands and beach front regions give fundamental visit focuses to transient birds, connecting far off territories in a worldwide organization.

Past supporting earthbound life, water bodies harbor exceptional and particular environments. Coral reefs, tracked down in the warm and shallow waters of tropical seas, are focal points of biodiversity. The many-sided beneficial interaction among corals and green growth shapes the premise of these biological systems, making a sensitive equilibrium that supports a horde of marine life. The soundness of coral reefs is complicatedly attached to the nature of water, as contaminations, increasing temperatures, and sea fermentation present huge dangers to their sensitive harmony.

In freshwater environments, the presence of wetlands adds to water cleaning and supplement cycling. Wetlands go about as regular channels, catching dregs and poisons, and assume a fundamental part in keeping up with water quality. The capacity of wetlands to retain overabundance water during floods and delivery it during dry periods gives a characteristic cushion against limits in hydrological conditions. These environments, frequently underestimated, convey fundamental administrations that add to the general strength of scenes and the prosperity of human networks.

The ensemble of nature organized by water bodies stretches out to the air domain. Lakes and seas, with their immense surface regions, assume a critical part in managing environment designs.

Vanishing from these water bodies discharges water fume into the environment, adding to the development of mists and precipitation. The appropriation of intensity and dampness all over the planet, driven by sea flows and environmental course, shapes atmospheric conditions and impacts territorial environments.

The unpredictable dance of water and environment is exemplified in peculiarities like El Niño and La Niña. These environment designs, portrayed by varieties in ocean surface temperatures in the Pacific Sea, have sweeping consequences for weather patterns around the world. From dry spells to floods, the effects of these peculiarities feature the interconnectedness of water bodies and environment frameworks. Understanding these connections is critical for anticipating and alleviating the impacts of environmental change on water assets and biological systems.

As the ensemble of nature unfurls, human exercises arise as a critical note, impacting the congruity or disunity of water bodies. Urbanization, industrialization, and horticultural practices bring contaminations into water frameworks, modifying their structure and compromising the soundness of oceanic environments. Overflow from cleared surfaces conveys contaminations like oil, weighty metals, and synthetic compounds into streams and lakes, compromising water quality and influencing the living beings that rely upon these natural surroundings.

The interest for water assets by developing human populaces represents extra difficulties. Extreme extraction of water from streams and springs for farming, industry, and homegrown use can prompt the consumption of water bodies. The adjustment of regular stream designs, like the development of dams and levees, can upset biological systems and influence the relocation of oceanic species. Finding some kind of harmony between human necessities and the protection of water biological systems turns into a basic thought in economical water the executives.

Environmental change further intensifies these difficulties, presenting vulnerabilities and fueling existing weights on water bodies. Changes in precipitation designs, expanded recurrence of outrageous climate occasions, and climbing temperatures all add to the perplexing elements of water frameworks. Adjusting to these progressions requires an all encompassing methodology that thinks about the interconnectedness of biological systems, the job of water in environment guideline, and the basic of economical asset the board.

Despite these difficulties, protection and reclamation endeavors arise as key instruments in saving the amicability of water bodies. The security of riparian zones, the execution of economical fishing rehearses, and the decrease of contamination inputs all add to keeping up with the strength of water biological systems. The reclamation of wetlands, which go about as regular channels and give fundamental territory, turns into a need in moderating the effects of human exercises.

Local area commitment and mindfulness assume a pivotal part in these protection endeavors. Teaching people and networks about the worth of water environments, the significance of mindful water use, and the outcomes of contamination encourages a feeling of stewardship. Resident science drives, affecting individuals in checking and information assortment, contribute significant data for understanding the condition of water bodies and carrying out powerful preservation systems.

Developments in innovation additionally offer apparatuses for observing and overseeing water assets. Remote detecting innovations, for example, give significant information on the state of water bodies, assisting with distinguishing patterns and survey the effect of human exercises. High level water treatment advances add to the sanitization of dirtied water, offering answers for relieving the impacts of defilement. The combination of conventional natural information with present day logical methodologies improves how we might interpret the mind boggling elements of water biological systems.

The job of water bodies in molding the ensemble of nature is indivisible from the more extensive setting of planetary wellbeing. The interconnectedness of water, biodiversity, environment, and human exercises highlights the requirement for incorporated ways to deal with preservation and maintainable administration. The Unified Countries' Economical Advancement Objectives, including Objective 6: Clean Water and Sterilization, stress the significance of guaranteeing the accessibility and feasible administration of water and disinfection for all.

6.2 Discuss the importance of rivers, lakes, and oceans in supporting life.

The significance of streams, lakes, and seas in supporting life on Earth is tremendous, as these waterways comprise fundamental parts of the planet's biological systems. Every one of these water sources assumes a remarkable part in cultivating biodiversity, managing environment, and supporting different living things, from minute organic entities to huge marine well evolved creatures. Understanding their importance reveals the complicated snare of associations that make Earth a dynamic and tenable planet.

Waterways, with their streaming waters and dynamic courses, act as helps for innumerable species. They are not simply topographical highlights but rather imperative passageways that shape scenes, impact biological systems, and give fundamental assets to both earthly and oceanic life. The cadenced progression of streams guarantees the vehicle of supplements, silt, and natural matter, enhancing the encompassing area and making rich environments for different widely varied vegetation.

The biodiversity upheld by waterways is shocking, including a great many animal types adjusted to different sea-going conditions. Fish, specifically, flourish in the powerful states of waterway biological systems.

Salmon, for example, set out on incredible relocations from freshwater streams to the vast sea and back, adding to the development of supplements and molding both riverine and marine environments. The perplexing life patterns of waterway staying organic entities feature the interconnectedness of earthly and amphibian territories.

Lakes, described by still or slow-streaming waters, address extraordinary environments with their own natural elements. They go about as supplies of freshwater, giving fundamental food to different organic entities. The quiet surfaces of lakes act as mirrors, mirroring the encompassing scenes and adding to the tasteful excellence of regular habitats. From minuscule green growth to enormous fish and waterfowl, lakes support a different exhibit of life, every species assuming a part in the complex equilibrium of the environment.

Wetlands, frequently connected with lakeshores and riverbanks, are dynamic and biodiverse environments that add to the soundness of water bodies. These momentary zones among oceanic and earthbound conditions give essential environment to creatures of land and water, waterfowl, and a heap of plant animal categories. Wetlands go about as regular channels, catching poisons and dregs, and assume an essential part in water filtration. Their capacity to store and gradually discharge water mitigates floods and dry seasons, offering extra advantages to encompassing scenes.

Seas, covering most of the World's surface, are the biggest and most compelling waterways on earth. They are not just home to a stunning assortment of marine life yet additionally assume a principal part in forming worldwide environment designs. The seas go about as an immense supply of intensity, retaining and conveying sun powered energy across the planet. Sea flows, driven by temperature and saltiness slopes, control environment by rearranging warmth and impacting climate frameworks.

The biodiversity found in seas is unrivaled, going from tiny microscopic fish to titanic whales. Coral reefs, frequently alluded to as the rainforests of the ocean, are focal points of marine life, supporting a staggering variety of species. The cooperative connection among corals and green growth frames the groundwork of these environments, making a fragile equilibrium that supports a perplexing trap of collaborations.

Mangrove timberlands, tracked down in waterfront regions, give fundamental living space to various species and go about as nurseries for fish and spineless creatures.

The significance of seas in supporting life stretches out past the marine climate. Phytoplankton, minuscule photosynthetic creatures, produce a huge part of the world's oxygen and structure the foundation of the marine food web. Zooplankton, thusly, give a vital connection among phytoplankton and bigger marine living beings. The many-sided connections inside sea biological systems, from the minute to the gigantic, add to the general wellbeing and equilibrium of the planet.

Streams, lakes, and seas are essential parts of the water cycle, a crucial interaction that supports life on The planet. Vanishing from the surfaces of these water bodies adds to the development of mists, which, thusly, discharge precipitation back to the land. This interminable cycle guarantees the accessibility of freshwater for earthly environments, rural exercises, and human networks. The strength of water bodies straightforwardly impacts the appropriation and wealth of precipitation, making them fundamental players in the guideline of environment.

Human social orders have flourished along the banks of waterways and shores of lakes and seas for centuries. The accessibility of freshwater for farming, drinking, and transportation has molded the improvement of civilizations. Stream valleys, like those of the Nile, Tigris and Euphrates, and the Indus, have been supports of old societies, giving prolific soil and solid water hotspots for horticulture. Ports along shorelines have been centers of exchange and trade, associating far off districts and cultivating social trade.

The significance of waterways, lakes, and seas in supporting life is personally connected to the idea of environment administrations. These waterways give a huge number of administrations that add to human prosperity. Freshwater from streams and lakes is an essential wellspring of drinking water for billions of individuals around the world. The richness of waterway valleys and lake shores upholds horticulture, giving fundamental food assets. Seas, with their tremendous fisheries, contribute essentially to worldwide protein utilization.

Past direct human advantages, water bodies offer sporting open doors, tasteful worth, and social importance. Lakeshores give peaceful settings to recreation exercises, and riverbanks frequently act as normal hallways for climbing and investigation. Seaside regions, with their sandy sea shores and lively marine life, draw in vacationers and encourage an association with the regular world. Many societies all over the planet have created otherworldly and social practices based on waterways, lakes, and seas, perceiving their inborn worth past utilitarian purposes.

In any case, the meaning of these water bodies faces phenomenal difficulties in the contemporary period. Human exercises, including industrialization, urbanization, and farming escalation, have prompted contamination and natural surroundings annihilation in many water biological systems. Overflow from farming fields brings manures and pesticides into streams and lakes, influencing water quality and amphibian life.

Metropolitan regions, with their impenetrable surfaces, add to expanded overflow and change regular stream designs.

Environmental change represents one more considerable danger to the strength of waterways, lakes, and seas. Climbing temperatures, ocean level ascent, and changes in precipitation designs straightforwardly influence the physical and synthetic properties of water bodies. Coral reefs, currently defenseless against dying because of temperature stress, face further difficulties as seas warm. Liquefying ice covers and glacial masses add to changes in stream designs, influencing freshwater accessibility and biodiversity in riverine environments.

The exhaustion of fisheries in seas due to overfishing represents a danger to the sensitive equilibrium of marine biological systems. Impractical fishing rehearses, for example, fishing and bycatch, have prompted decreases in fish populaces and disturbances in food networks. The deficiency of biodiversity in water bodies has broad outcomes, influencing the living beings straightforwardly affected as well as the administrations these biological systems give to mankind.

Protection and reasonable administration of waterways, lakes, and seas are basic for keeping up with their job in supporting life. Drives pointed toward safeguarding water quality, reestablishing territories, and moderating the effects of environmental change are fundamental parts of such endeavors. The foundation of marine safeguarded regions, where human exercises are directed to limit damage to biological systems, is urgent for shielding the biodiversity of seas. Stream reclamation projects, including endeavors to eliminate dams and further develop water stream, add to the strength of riverine biological systems.

Worldwide joint effort is key in tending to the transboundary idea of many water-related difficulties. Shared waterway bowls and interconnected sea flows require composed endeavors among countries to oversee and safeguard these basic assets. Arrangements and arrangements, like the Unified Countries Show on the Law of the Ocean (UNCLOS) and provincial drives for water the board, give systems to collaboration and reasonable utilization of shared water bodies.

Schooling and mindfulness assume critical parts in encouraging a feeling of obligation and stewardship toward water bodies. Illuminating people group about the significance regarding streams, lakes, and seas, as well as the dangers they face, engages people to settle on informed decisions in their regular routines. Resident science drives, where individuals from the general population add to observing and research endeavors, upgrade how we might interpret water environments and backing preservation endeavors.

Innovative headways additionally add to the protection and feasible administration of water bodies. Remote detecting advances give important information to observing changes in the physical and organic qualities of seas. Developments in water treatment advancements assist with tending to contamination and guarantee the accessibility of clean freshwater. Coordinating conventional natural information with current logical methodologies improves how we might interpret the intricacies of water biological systems and illuminates compelling preservation procedures.

All in all, the significance of waterways, lakes, and seas in supporting life on Earth couldn't possibly be more significant. These waterways structure the complex strings that wind around together biological systems.

6.3 Explore the impact of human activities on water ecosystems and conservation efforts.

The effect of human exercises on water environments is significant and complex, going from contamination and territory obliteration to over-extraction of assets and environmental change. As the worldwide populace proceeds to develop and industrialization grows, the tensions on water biological systems increase, presenting critical difficulties to their wellbeing and maintainability. In equal, preservation endeavors endeavor to address these difficulties, trying to reestablish and safeguard water environments through a blend of strategy mediations, mechanical developments, and local area commitment.

Contamination, coming about because of different human exercises, remains as one of the most inescapable dangers to water biological systems. Rural overflow, conveying pesticides and composts, enters streams and lakes, prompting supplement awkward nature and algal blossoms. These blossoms can exhaust oxygen levels in the water, causing "no man's lands" where marine life can't get by. Urbanization adds to non-point source contamination, with stormwater overflow conveying poisons from streets and impenetrable surfaces into water bodies. Modern releases discharge weighty metals, synthetics, and poisons into streams and seas, further compromising water quality.

The effect of contamination stretches out past the quick oceanic climate to influence human networks that depend on these water sources. Defiled water presents dangers to general wellbeing, prompting waterborne illnesses and long haul medical problems. In addition, the corruption of water quality upsets fisheries, compromises drinking water supplies, and reduces the stylish and sporting worth of water bodies. Tending to water contamination requires thorough procedures, including the authorization of natural guidelines, the execution of economical farming practices, and the advancement of innovations for water treatment.

Environment obliteration, driven by exercises like deforestation, metropolitan extension, and framework improvement, represents a huge danger to the biodiversity of water biological systems. Wetlands, urgent environments that give favorable places to numerous species and go about as regular channels, are frequently depleted or filled for agrarian and metropolitan turn of events. Stream channels are modified through dam development, influencing the regular progression of water and blocking the movement of fish. Waterfront regions, wealthy in biodiversity and fundamental for marine life, face territory misfortune because of beach front turn of events and ocean level ascent.

The change of environments disturbs the perplexing associations inside biological systems, prompting decreases in species variety and overflow. Amphibian living beings that rely upon explicit territories, for example, riverbank vegetation or coral reefs, find their homes decreased or obliterated. Transitory species, similar to salmon and ocean turtles, face hindrances in their excursions as normal halls are deterred.

The deficiency of biodiversity in water biological systems has flowing impacts, affecting environment capabilities, flexibility, and the administrations they give to human networks.

Over-extraction of water assets for horticulture, industry, and civil use intensifies the weight on water environments. Streams and springs are tapped past their economical yields, prompting diminished water levels, adjusted stream designs, and the debasement of sea-going natural surroundings. Groundwater exhaustion influences the soundness of wetlands and springs, basic parts of water scenes. The exorbitant withdrawal of water for water system can bring about soil salinization and a decrease in water quality.

The outcomes of over-extraction reach out past the sea-going domain, influencing earthbound environments and human social orders. Decreased water accessibility imperils rural efficiency, prompting food uncertainty and financial difficulties. Groundwater consumption adds to land subsidence, a peculiarity saw in districts vigorously dependent on springs. The interconnection between surface water and groundwater highlights the requirement for coordinated water the board methodologies that focus on supportability and think about the effects on both oceanic and earthly conditions.

Environmental change, driven by human-actuated ozone depleting substance emanations, represents extra dangers to water biological systems. Climbing temperatures impact precipitation designs, prompting changes in the recurrence and force of outrageous climate occasions. Expanded temperatures and adjusted precipitation add to dry seasons and floods, affecting water accessibility and quality. The warming of seas prompts coral blanching, influencing the soundness of coral reefs. Ocean level ascent infringes upon seaside territories, worsening the deficiency of basic biological systems.

The effects of environmental change are not segregated; they cooperate with different stressors, enhancing the difficulties looked by water biological systems. For example, a hotter environment can compound the impacts of contamination by increasing supplement overflow and advancing destructive algal blossoms. The versatility of oceanic species to changing circumstances is compromised, prompting shifts in conveyance and potential populace declines. Adjusting to these progressions requires an all encompassing methodology that thinks about the interconnected idea of natural stressors and their combined consequences for water environments.

Preservation endeavors mean to relieve the effects of human exercises on water biological systems and shield their natural uprightness. These endeavors include a scope of methodologies and mediations that address contamination, natural surroundings misfortune, over-extraction, and environmental change.

Natural strategies and guidelines assume an essential part in forming manageable practices and forestalling further debasement of water bodies. Severe norms for water quality, discharges, and land use guide ventures and networks towards mindful stewardship.

Advancements in innovation add to preservation endeavors by giving devices to checking, evaluation, and rebuilding of water environments. High level water treatment advancements assist with moderating contamination by eliminating toxins from wastewater. Remote detecting advances, satellite symbolism, and geographic data frameworks (GIS) empower researchers and traditionalists to follow changes in water quality, living space misfortune, and land use. The combination of huge information and computerized reasoning improves our capacity to demonstrate and foresee the effects of human exercises on water environments.

Reclamation projects look to restore debased water biological systems and upgrade their strength to ecological stressors. Endeavors to reestablish riverbanks, wetlands, and beach front regions include establishing local vegetation, eliminating obtrusive species, and carrying out disintegration control measures. Dam evacuation projects, when environmentally practical, mean to reestablish normal stream designs and resuscitate territories for transitory fish. Coral reef rebuilding drives convey methods, for example, coral transplantation and fake designs to advance reef recuperation.

Environment based ways to deal with water the executives perceive the interconnectedness of normal frameworks and human exercises. Incorporated watershed the executives plans think about the whole scene, representing the wellsprings of contamination, the wellbeing of waterway environments, and the requirements of nearby networks. Preservation specialists work with partners, including neighborhood networks, enterprises, and policymakers, to create and carry out methodologies that offset human requirements with the natural soundness of water scenes.

Worldwide coordinated effort is vital for tending to the transboundary idea of many water-related difficulties. Shared waterway bowls, seaside zones, and interconnected sea flows require helpful endeavors among countries. Settlements and arrangements, like the Ramsar Show on Wetlands and the Show on Natural Variety, give structures to global participation in the preservation and supportable utilization of water biological systems. Worldwide drives, like the Supportable Improvement Objectives (SDGs), highlight the significance of coordinated water the executives in accomplishing more extensive natural and social targets.

Local area commitment and training assume urgent parts in cultivating a culture of preservation and reasonable water use. Enabling nearby networks to become stewards of their water assets includes bringing issues to light about the significance of water environments, the dangers they face, and the job people can play in preservation. Resident science drives empower public support in checking and information assortment, improving comprehension we might interpret neighborhood water environments and illuminating protection endeavors.

Water preservation rehearses at the individual and local area levels add to diminishing the interest for water assets. Productive water use in agribusiness, industry, and families limits the effect on water environments. Advances, for example, dribble water system, water collecting, and water-proficient machines assist with upgrading water use. Instructive missions and effort programs support capable water utilization and waste decrease, advancing a feeling of shared liability regarding the wellbeing of water biological systems.

The perplexing trap of water biological systems, containing streams, lakes, and seas, is fundamental for the wellbeing and equilibrium of our planet. These environments are wellsprings of life as well as controllers of environment, suppliers of biological system administrations, and natural surroundings for an exceptional variety of species. Nonetheless, the persistent development of human exercises has essentially modified these fragile conditions, presenting extreme dangers to their supportability. Preservation endeavors, driven by a mix of strategy drives, mechanical developments, and local area commitment, endeavor to address the effects of human exercises and guarantee the flexibility of water biological systems for people in the future.

Human Effect on Water Environments:

Contamination:

One of the most inescapable and harming impacts of human exercises on water environments is contamination. Horticultural spillover, conveying pesticides and manures, invades streams and lakes, causing supplement irregular characteristics and advancing algal blossoms. These blossoms lead to oxygen consumption, making no man's lands where marine life can't get by. Urbanization adds to non-point source contamination, as stormwater overflow conveys poisons from streets and impenetrable surfaces into water bodies. Modern releases discharge weighty metals, synthetic compounds, and poisons, further compromising water quality.

The repercussions of contamination reach out past oceanic conditions to influence human wellbeing and prosperity. Polluted water sources present dangers of waterborne infections, influencing networks that depend on these biological systems for drinking water and means. Furthermore, the corruption of water quality adversely impacts fisheries, compromising food security and monetary steadiness. The stylish and sporting worth of water bodies are reduced as contamination changes immaculate waters into corrupted conditions.

Territory Obliteration:

Human-incited natural surroundings obliteration is another basic element adding to the downfall of water biological systems. Wetlands, fundamental for biodiversity and water filtration, are depleted or filled for horticultural extension and metropolitan turn of events. Waterway channels are adjusted through dam development, disturbing regular stream designs and impeding the relocation of fish. Waterfront regions, wealthy in biodiversity and vital for marine life, face living space misfortune because of beach front turn of events and rising ocean levels.

The obliteration of these territories upsets the complex equilibrium inside environments, prompting decreases in species variety and overflow. Species subject to explicit natural surroundings, for example, riverbank vegetation or coral reefs, face difficulties as their homes are decreased or obliterated. Transitory species, similar to salmon and ocean turtles, experience snags in their excursions as regular hallways are discouraged. The deficiency of biodiversity in water environments has flowing impacts, affecting biological system capabilities, strength, and the administrations they give to human networks.

Over-Extraction of Assets:

The over-extraction of water assets for horticulture, industry, and metropolitan use fuels the weight on water environments. Streams and springs are tapped past their maintainable yields, prompting diminished water levels, changed stream designs, and the debasement of sea-going territories. Groundwater consumption influences the strength of wetlands and springs, basic parts of water scenes. Exorbitant withdrawal of water for water system can bring about soil salinization and a decrease in water quality.

The results of over-extraction stretch out past the oceanic domain, influencing earthly biological systems and human social orders. Decreased water accessibility imperils farming efficiency, prompting food instability and monetary difficulties. Groundwater consumption adds to land subsidence, a peculiarity saw in districts vigorously dependent on springs. The interconnection between surface water and groundwater highlights the requirement for incorporated water the board procedures that focus on maintainability and think about the effects on both sea-going and earthbound conditions.

Environmental Change:

Human-prompted environmental change represents extra dangers to water biological systems. Climbing temperatures impact precipitation designs, prompting changes in the recurrence and power of outrageous climate occasions. Expanded temperatures and changed precipitation add to dry seasons and floods, influencing water accessibility and quality. The warming of seas prompts coral dying, influencing the strength of coral reefs. Ocean level ascent infringes upon beach front natural surroundings, intensifying the deficiency of basic biological systems.

The effects of environmental change communicate with different stressors, enhancing the difficulties looked by water biological systems. For example, a hotter environment can worsen the impacts of contamination by escalating supplement overflow and advancing hurtful algal sprouts. The versatility of oceanic species to changing circumstances is compromised, prompting shifts in circulation and potential populace declines. Adjusting to these progressions requires a comprehensive methodology that thinks about the interconnected idea of natural stressors and their combined impacts on water environments.

Protection Endeavors:

Strategy and Guideline:

Ecological strategies and guidelines assume an essential part in forming maintainable practices and forestalling further debasement of water bodies. State run administrations and global bodies execute tough guidelines for water quality, outflows, and land use, directing ventures and networks toward dependable stewardship. The foundation of safeguarded regions and preservation zones helps protect basic environments, guaranteeing that human exercises are managed to limit mischief to biological systems.

Worldwide joint effort is vital for address the transboundary idea of many water-related difficulties. Shared stream bowls, seaside zones, and interconnected sea ebbs and flows require agreeable endeavors among countries. Arrangements and arrangements, like the Ramsar Show on Wetlands and the Show on Natural Variety, give systems to global collaboration in the preservation and economical utilization of water environments. Worldwide drives, like the Feasible Improvement Objectives (SDGs), highlight the significance of coordinated water the board in accomplishing more extensive natural and social goals.

Mechanical Developments:

Developments in innovation assume a critical part in propelling protection endeavors for water biological systems. High level water treatment innovations assist with relieving contamination by eliminating foreign substances from wastewater. Remote detecting advancements, satellite symbolism, and geographic data frameworks (GIS) empower researchers and traditionalists to follow changes in water quality, territory misfortune, and land use. The joining of huge information and man-made consciousness improves our capacity to demonstrate and foresee the effects of human exercises on water environments.

These innovative instruments enable preservation experts with important data for independent direction and asset distribution. Constant checking of water quality considers fast reactions to contamination occurrences, limiting the degree of harm to biological systems. Geographic data frameworks give spatial experiences, supporting the ID of basic territories and regions requiring preservation intercessions. Mechanical advancements keep on developing, offering new answers for the difficulties looked by water environments in the cutting edge time.

Rebuilding Tasks:

Rebuilding projects mean to restore corrupted water biological systems and improve their flexibility to natural stressors. Endeavors to reestablish riverbanks, wetlands, and waterfront regions include establishing local vegetation, eliminating obtrusive species, and carrying out disintegration control measures. Dam expulsion projects, when biologically practical, plan to reestablish normal stream designs and restore living spaces for transitory fish. Coral reef rebuilding drives send strategies, for example, coral transplantation and fake designs to advance reef recuperation.

Environment based ways to deal with water the executives perceive the interconnectedness of normal frameworks and human exercises. Coordinated watershed the board plans think about the whole scene, representing the wellsprings of contamination, the soundness of stream environments, and the necessities of nearby networks. Protection specialists work with partners, including neighborhood networks, businesses, and policymakers, to create and execute methodologies that offset human requirements with the natural wellbeing of water scenes.

Local area Commitment and Schooling:

Local area commitment and schooling assume vital parts in cultivating a culture of preservation and feasible water use. Enabling nearby networks to become stewards of their water assets includes bringing issues to light about the significance of water biological systems, the dangers they face, and the job people can play in protection. Resident science drives support public cooperation in checking and information assortment, improving comprehension we might interpret neighborhood water environments and illuminating preservation endeavors.

Instructive missions and effort programs at nearby and worldwide levels add to building a feeling of obligation and shared obligation to water preservation. Understanding the many-sided connections inside water biological systems encourages appreciation for the worth of spotless and sound water bodies. By effectively including networks in preservation drives, there is an improved probability of fruitful execution and long haul maintainability of protection endeavors.

Water Protection Practices:

Water preservation rehearses at the individual and local area levels add to decreasing the interest for water assets. Proficient water use in farming, industry, and families limits the effect on water environments. Advances, for example, dribble water system, water gathering, and water-effective machines assist with enhancing water use.

Chapter 7

The Song of the Sky - Birds and Beyond

In the immense breadth of the sky, where the sky blue material meets the earth in a timeless hug, an ensemble of life unfurls. This is the Tune of the Sky, a pleasant embroidery woven by the endless animals that call the sky their home. Among these, the birds stand apart as the maestros, the virtuosos of this divine ensemble.

As sunrise breaks, the main notes of the orchestra arise. The sun, a brilliant guide, raises its cudgel, and the sky starts to murmur with the enlivening of the avian world. The birds, with plumes of bunch tints, take off, their wings slicing through the air like notes on a melodic staff. From the treetops to the open skies, their voices ascend as one, making an agreeable suggestion that declares the appearance of another day.

Every species contributes its exceptional tone to this heavenly organization. The songbird, with its merry quaver, proclaims the morning, while the robin adds a lively whistle to the chorale. The cawing of crows and the cooing of birds give a bass and alto, establishing the song in the earth beneath. High over, the glorious falcon takes off, its sharp eyes reviewing the scene as it adds a majestic rhythm to the creation.

However, the avian ensemble isn't restricted to the sunshine hours. As the sun slides into the great beyond, another development starts. Nighttime birds, with eyes adjusted to the shadowiness, become the dominant focal point. The hoot of the owl reverberations through the quiet evening, joined by the unpleasant calls of nightjars. Bats, the concealed artists, participate with their echolocation, making a musical background to the divine presentation.

However, past the recognizable avian voices, there are different sounds that add to the Melody of the Sky. The stirring of leaves as a delicate breeze moves throughout the branches, the far off thunder of thunder proclaiming a coming tempest, and the musical patter of raindrops on leaves — this large number of components mesh into the rich embroidery of the sky's tune.

As people, we are advantaged audience members to this fabulous orchestra. We look upwards, enraptured by the mind boggling dance of the birds, the moving mists, and the always changing tones of the sky. In our endeavor to comprehend and associate with this divine exhibition, we have appointed implications to the examples and ways of behaving of the avian craftsmen.

Old societies viewed birds as couriers from the heavenly, their flight an extension between the natural domain and the sky above. The hawk, with its taking off wings, represented strength and mental fortitude, while the bird turned into an insignia of harmony. Fantasies and legends were made around the birds, and their way of behaving was deciphered as signs and signs.

In the cutting edge period, our interest with birds has not decreased; rather, it has developed. Ornithologists and birdwatchers furnished with optics and handle guides leave on journeys to notice and report the different species that effortlessness the skies. The language of science has joined the idyllic understandings of old, as specialists look to disentangle the secrets of avian relocation, correspondence, and knowledge.

Birdsong, as well, has turned into a subject of logical request. Ornithologists concentrate on the complicated examples and varieties in avian vocalizations, endeavoring to translate the messages encoded in the melodic expressions. The songbird's melody, when the motivation for writers and performers, is presently dissected for its complicated construction and the data it passes on to possible mates.

However, even with our logical comprehension, there stays a component of secret in the Melody of the Sky. The movements of birds across tremendous distances, directed by an inborn ability to know east from west, evade total clarification. The perplexing examples of murmurations, where rushes of starlings move as one, make hypnotizing shows that resist simple perception.

As we dive further into the privileged insights of the avian world, we find that the Melody of the Sky stretches out past the world's environment. The heavenly bodies themselves become piece of this grandiose ensemble.

The musical dance of the planets, the frightful calls of pulsars, and the infinite murmur of the universe contribute their own tunes to the fantastic creation of presence.

In our investigation of the universe, we have sent messengers — space tests that navigate the boundlessness of room, conveying with them the reverberations of human interest. These counterfeit couriers, similar to the birds of Earth, sing their own melody as they venture through the grandiose territory. The signs they communicate back to us, encoded in the language of science, become piece of the steadily growing collection of the Tune of the Sky.

As we ponder the magnificence of the sky, we are reminded that our association with the sky goes past the physical. The Melody of the Sky resounds with our feelings, summoning a feeling of miracle, wonder, and, on occasion, contemplation. The changing shades of the dusk might mix sensations of serenity, while the thunder of thunder might inspire a basic feeling of fervor and veneration.

In the quiet of the evening, when the stars sparkle like heavenly notes on a grandiose staff, we might track down comfort in the limitlessness of the universe. The star groupings above, named and envisioned by societies since the beginning of time, become a divine guide that directs our thought of the boundless. The Smooth Way, a brilliant waterway of stars, coaxes us to consider the secrets that lie past the limits of our comprehension.

In the advanced time, our relationship with the sky has taken on new aspects. Urbanization and fake light have modified the nighttime scene, projecting a cloak over the splendor of the stars. Light contamination, a result of our innovative advancement, takes steps to darken the divine notes of the evening, muting the voices of the nighttime birds and quieting the murmurs of the universe.

However, even amidst these difficulties, there is trust. Preservation endeavors and mindfulness crusades try to save the dim skies and safeguard the living spaces of the avian entertainers. Networks meet up to praise the marvels of the night sky, arranging stargazing occasions that reconnect individuals with the heavenly songs that have roused mankind for centuries.

As we explore the intricacies of the cutting edge world, the Melody of the Sky turns into a wellspring of motivation and reflection. The birds, with their wings outstretched and voices raised, help us to remember the vast potential outcomes that lie into the great beyond. The evolving seasons, set apart by the movements of birds and the dance of groups of stars, offer a musicality that grounds us in the repeating idea of life.

In our quest for progress, may we not fail to remember the significance of safeguarding the Tune of the Sky. The fragile equilibrium of biological systems, the transient courses of birds, and the lucidity of the night sky — this large number of components add to the agreeable song that resounds through the universe. As stewards of the earth, it is our obligation to guarantee that this heavenly ensemble perseveres for a long time into the future.

In the calm snapshots of reflection, as we look upwards and lose ourselves in the endlessness of the sky, let us recall that we are nevertheless one note in the terrific structure of presence. The birds, with their vaporous flights and ageless tunes, show us the magnificence of living as one with the regular world. The divine bodies, with their quiet dance across the infinite stage, help us to remember the interconnectedness, everything being equal.

Thus, under the open sky, in the midst of the stirring leaves and the calls of birds, we wind up encompassed in the Tune of the Sky. A song rises above reality, an orchestra that repeats the excellence of creation. As we pay attention to its consistently evolving notes, may we be enlivened to appreciate and safeguard the valuable endowment of the sky — the material on which the Melody of the Sky unfurls in the entirety of its superb brilliance.

7.1 Focus on the avian contributions to the silent symphony.

In the terrific embroidery of the regular world, the avian commitments to the quiet orchestra stand apart as a demonstration of the magnificence and variety of life. Birds, with their complicated plumage, smooth flight, and charming tunes, assume a urgent part in forming the environmental song that encompasses us. From the day break melody to the nighttime serenades, their voices mesh consistently into the texture of the regular soundscape.

At the core of the avian commitment is the morning chorale — an agreeable suggestion that declares the appearance of another day. As the principal light breaks not too far off, a bunch of birds from different species participate in this aggregate execution. Every species, with its interesting vocalizations, adds a layer to the ensemble, making a clamor of sounds that reverberate through the air.

The sweet quaver of the songbird, roosted on an influencing branch, pierces the quietness of the early morning. Its tune, a festival of the rising sun, fills in as a clarion call to different birds to participate in the chorale. The robin, with its merry whistle, adds a perky rhythm, while the blackbird contributes a rich, woodwind like tune. Together, they make an intricate and dynamic sythesis that reflects the lively life arousing with the sunrise.

The avian ensemble isn't bound to a particular classification; rather, it traverses a range of sounds and styles. The songbirds, with their quick and mind boggling tunes, participate in a melodic exchange that appears to echo through the foliage.

The cadenced tapping of woodpeckers on tree trunks gives a percussive component, interspersing the avian presentation with staccato beats. The jays, with their rambunctious calls, present a strong and confident subject to the ensemble.

As the day unfurls, the avian commitments keep on advancing. The ethereal tumbling of swallows, swifts, and martins add a powerful aspect to the sky. Their dipping and jumping make a visual movement that supplements their piercing calls, reverberating through the open spaces. The quick, with its smoothed out structure, appears to slice through the air like a bolt, abandoning a path of melodic notes.

In the thick foliage, the secret entertainers — the warblers — become the dominant focal point. The songbird, prestigious for its rich and musical melody, serenades the dusk hours. Its frightful notes, conveyed with accuracy and feeling, dazzle the audience and inspire a feeling of marvel. The thrush, roosted in the underbrush, adds a woodwind like quality to the night tune, consuming the space with ethereal harmonies.

However, it is the aggregate exertion of the avian local area that changes the normal world into a living ensemble. The sparrows, humble for all intents and purposes, contribute a consistent foundation murmur, making a sonic embroidery that ties the different components of the avian symphony together. Their presence is an update that each specie, regardless of how normal, assumes a fundamental part in the unpredictable equilibrium of the biological system.

As day gives way to night, another development in the avian orchestra arises. The nighttime birds, with their transformations to low light circumstances, assume control over the stage. The eerie calls of owls resound through the haziness, their hoots and shrieks reverberating across the quiet scene. Nightjars, with their particular churring sounds, add a secretive and powerful quality to the evening.

Bats, albeit not birds, additionally add to the nighttime ensemble. Their ultrasonic calls, past the scope of human hearing, make a mind boggling and musical foundation commotion as they explore during that time sky. These imperceptible entertainers, directed by echolocation, carry another layer to the ensemble, highlighting the variety of the avian and flying commitments to the quiet symphony.

The avian ensemble isn't restricted to a particular geographic area; rather, it is a worldwide peculiarity. From the thick rainforests of the Amazon to the immense tundras of the Cold, birds adjust their melodies and ways of behaving to their one of a kind conditions. The lyrebird of Australia, an expert of mimicry, integrates the hints of different birds, creatures, and even hardware into its collection. The ptarmigan of the Icy, covered in its cold living space, discharges delicate clacking sounds that mix consistently with the frozen scene.

Relocation, a surprising avian peculiarity, adds one more layer to the ensemble. The sounding of relocating geese, flying in Angular developments across the sky, is a sign of the evolving seasons. The sandpipers, with their piercing calls, set out on legendary excursions, crossing mainlands and seas looking for reasonable favorable places. The synchronized flight and vocalizations of these transitory birds make a scene that rises above borders and interfaces far off scenes.

In the domain of avian correspondence, the language of birdsong becomes the overwhelming focus. Every species has its own collection of vocalizations, going from basic peeps to intricate and sweet melodies. The reason for these melodies goes past simple tasteful articulation; they act for the purpose of correspondence, passing messages related on to an area, romance, and admonitions.

The sunrise chorale, for instance, isn't simply an irregular explosion of tune; it is an essential correspondence technique utilized by male birds to lay out and shield their regions. The strong singing of a male bird fills in as both a solicitation to likely mates and an admonition to equal guys. The complicated examples and varieties in birdsong pass on data about the wellbeing, wellness, and hereditary ability of the vocalist.

Romance ceremonies, frequently joined by intricate presentations of plumage and melody, further feature the significance of avian correspondence in the regular world. The complicated moves of cranes, the showy presentations of birds of heaven, and the synchronized trips of seeking birds all act as visual and hear-able signs in the perplexing dance of generation. The female, knowing and specific, assesses these presentations to pick a mate who can serious areas of strength for contribute to the future.

Past the domain of romance, birdsong likewise assumes a significant part in parental consideration and social cooperations. The asking calls of hungry chicks brief guardians to give sustenance, while contact calls assist with keeping up with union inside a herd. Some bird species participate in two part harmonies, where male and female accomplices orchestrate their vocalizations as a type of holding and correspondence. The complexities of these avian discussions uncover the refinement of the quiet orchestra that wraps the regular world.

With regards to avian insight, the capacity of certain birds to copy sounds and, surprisingly, human discourse adds a charming layer to the quiet ensemble. The well known lyrebird, tracked down in the woods of Australia, can mirror a wide exhibit of sounds, including trimming tools, camera screens, and vehicle cautions. Parrots, prestigious for their vocal mimicry, can learn and duplicate human discourse with noteworthy precision.

The mental capacities of birds stretch out past simple mimicry. A few animal categories, like crows and ravens, are known for their critical thinking abilities and device use.

The New Caledonian crow, specifically, has exhibited the capacity to specialty and use apparatuses to remove bugs from tree covering — an illustration of avian inventiveness that challenges customary ideas of creature insight.

As we dig further into the universe of birdsong and avian correspondence, innovation turns into a partner in disentangling the intricacies of the quiet orchestra. Bioacoustics, the investigation of the sounds created by living creatures, permits scientists to dissect and inventory the multifaceted examples of birdsong. High level recording hardware, combined with AI calculations, empowers the distinguishing proof and following of individual bird species in light of their vocalizations.

In the field of preservation, the investigation of avian commitments to the quiet ensemble takes on another criticalness. The downfall of bird populaces, driven by territory misfortune, environmental change, and other human-prompted factors, represents a danger to the sensitive equilibrium of the regular world. Ornithologists and traditionalists influence innovation to screen and evaluate the strength of bird populaces, involving acoustic observing to follow changes in species creation and conduct.

Resident science projects, where lovers contribute their perceptions and accounts, assume a critical part in this undertaking. These resident researchers become ministers for the avian world, utilizing their energy and information to bring issues to light about the significance of birds and their commitments to the quiet orchestra. The aggregate endeavors of specialists, moderates, and resident researchers add to a more profound comprehension of the avian domain and the pressing need to safeguard it.

The avian orchestra, in any case, faces difficulties in the advanced world. Urbanization, territory discontinuity, and contamination disturb the regular rhythms and examples of birdlife. Counterfeit light around evening time, an outcome of metropolitan turn of events, impedes the way of behaving of nighttime birds and disturbs their capacity to explore. Glass structures represent a danger to birds in flight, prompting impacts that outcome in injury or passing.

Environmental change, with its erratic weather conditions and modifications to biological systems, represents a significant danger to avian life. Transient birds, finely receptive to occasional changes, face difficulties as the planning of their processes may never again line up with the accessibility of food and settling destinations. The sensitive equilibrium that has supported the avian ensemble for centuries is presently under danger, and the repercussions stretch out past the domain of the birds to affect the whole snare of life.

Because of these difficulties, preservation drives and support endeavors try to moderate the effects of human exercises on avian populaces. Planning bird-accommodating engineering, carrying out lights-out programs in metropolitan regions during top movement periods, and laying out safeguarded regions.

7.2 Explore the migration patterns, nesting behaviors, and calls of birds.

In the multifaceted dance of life that unfurls across the huge material of our planet, the movement designs, settling ways of behaving, and calls of birds arise as convincing parts in the narrative of the regular world. Birds, with their wings outstretched and melodies lifted to the sky, set out on incredible excursions, construct many-sided settles, and convey through a different exhibit of vocalizations. These ways of behaving are not simple step by step processes for surviving; they are significant articulations of transformation and development that have molded the avian world over ages.

Movement, perhaps of the most striking peculiarity in the avian domain, is a demonstration of the unyielding soul of birds. Consistently, a large number of birds embrace fantastic excursions, crossing mainlands and seas looking for positive circumstances for taking care of and rearing. The examples of movement are essentially as shifted as the actual species, reflecting variations to the different biological systems they possess.

One of the most famous transient excursions is that of the Icy Tern. This amazing bird, known for its significant distance flights, leaves on a yearly journey from its Icy favorable places to the Antarctic and back. Covering a stunning distance of as much as 44,000 kilometers (27,000 miles) every way, the Cold Tern crosses the globe, exploring with noteworthy accuracy utilizing divine prompts, Earth's attractive field, and visual tourist spots.

Conversely, the bar-followed godwit, one more boss of significant distance movement, holds the record for the longest direct trip of any bird. This bold explorer covers roughly 11,000 kilometers (6,800 miles) in a solitary departure from Gold country to New Zealand. During this long distance race venture, the godwit depends on put away fat stores to fuel its direct flight, showing the surprising physiological transformations that empower such accomplishments of perseverance.

The examples of relocation are not restricted to really long voyagers. Numerous species show more limited movements, moving among reproducing and non-favorable places inside a similar landmass. The American Robin, for instance, moves between its favorable places in North America and wintering grounds in the southern US. These more limited movements, however less emotional than the cross-country travels, are regardless vital for the endurance of many bird species.

As birds explore these huge distances, they face heap difficulties, from antagonistic atmospheric conditions to predation and the danger of crashes with human-made structures. Preservation endeavors, for example, the foundation of transient halls and safeguarded regions, expect to relieve these difficulties and guarantee the protected entry of transitory birds.

By understanding the complexities of movement, specialists and progressives can attempt to save the essential living spaces that act as waypoints in the excursions of these avian drifters.

Settling ways of behaving, one more enthralling part of the avian world, exhibit the variety of techniques utilized by birds to guarantee the endurance of their posterity. Home development is an expertise sharpened north of millions of long periods of development, with every species adjusting its way to deal with the particular requests of its current circumstance and way of life.

The pendulum swings between the fastidious modelers and the shrewd developers in the avian world. Consider the intricate homes made by weaverbirds in Africa. These magnificent engineers fastidiously mesh strands of grass into perplexing, hanging structures that hang from the branches. The accuracy and intricacy of these homes serve not just as havens for the eggs and chicks yet additionally as showcases of the manufacturer's ability, drawing in likely mates.

On the opposite finish of the range are the moderate methodologies embraced by birds like the Killdeer. This ground-settling shorebird shuns the complexities of woven homes, rather saving its eggs in a shallow discouragement on the ground. The mottled eggs, looking like stones, mix consistently with the general climate, giving a type of disguise that safeguards them from hunters.

Tunnel settling seabirds, like puffins and petrels, adopt an alternate strategy out and out. These birds uncover tunnels in the dirt or utilize normal fissure in rough bluffs to make places of refuge for their eggs. The underground idea of these homes gives protection and security against the brutal components, permitting these species to flourish in their difficult beach front environments.

The development of settling ways of behaving is additionally interlaced with the existence history of birds. Altricial birds, brought into the world in a moderately lacking state, require broad parental consideration and security. Numerous warblers fall into this classification, and their homes frequently mirror a secret unpredictability. The cup-molded homes concealed in the parts of trees or the thick undergrowth act as supports for the sensitive hatchlings, shielding them until they are prepared to fledge.

Precocial birds, then again, hatch in a further developed state and are fit for free development not long after birth. Waterfowl, similar to ducks and geese, frequently construct settles near water sources. These homes, whether developed from reeds and grasses or just a shallow sorrow in the ground, give a protected climate to the precocial chicks to investigate their environmental factors.

The variety of settling ways of behaving reaches out to the domain of provincial settling, where enormous gatherings of birds assemble to raise in closeness. Provinces, laid out on islands or waterfront bluffs, offer security in larger groups, with the collective presence dissuading hunters. Seabird provinces, clamoring with action and bedlam, become dynamic center points of avian life during the rearing season.

Correspondence in the avian world rises above the visual domain, tracking down articulation in the bunch calls, melodies, and vocalizations that characterize the acoustic scene. Birds use vocalizations for various purposes, an including area safeguard, romance, and keeping up with social bonds. The rich embroidery of avian vocalizations adds profundity to the normal soundscape, giving a method for correspondence that is both mind boggling and nuanced.

One of the most reminiscent types of bird correspondence is the melody. Tunes, frequently connected with male birds, serve numerous capabilities, including domain foundation and drawing in mates. The Songbird, famous for its strong and resonant tune, changes the night into a material of charm. Each quaver and prosper conveys data about the vocalist's imperativeness and hereditary wellness, making the songbird's melody an amazing asset in the serious universe of avian romance.

The mimicry capacities of some bird species add a fascinating layer to the avian orchestra. The Lyrebird, local to Australia, is an unbelievable copy that consolidates the hints of different birds, creatures, and, surprisingly, mechanical commotions into its collection. This mimicry, combined with intricate presentations of tail feathers, fills in as a type of correspondence and romance, displaying the lyrebird's flexibility and knowledge.

The calls of birds are similarly different, going from straightforward twitters and screeches to complex examples that pass on data about food sources, hunters, and the presence of gatecrashers. Many birds use contact calls to keep up with union inside a group, guaranteeing that people stay associated in their developments and exercises. These calls, frequently unobtrusive and barely noticeable by human ears, structure the inconspicuous strings that tight spot avian networks together.

Caution calls, sharp and particular, assume a critical part in avian correspondence. At the point when a potential danger is recognized, a bird will produce a caution call to alarm others nearby. The particularity of these calls is striking, for certain species having unmistakable alerts for various kinds of hunters. This quick and facilitated reaction to peril features the productivity of avian correspondence and the significance of keeping up with cautiousness in the regular world.

Notwithstanding vocalizations, visual shows and non-verbal communication additionally add to avian correspondence. The romance moves of cranes, with their mind boggling advances and synchronized developments, are a visual exhibition that passes on data about the wellness and wellbeing of likely mates. The intricate presentations of birds of heaven, enhanced with energetic plumage and participating in mind boggling moves, act as both visual and hear-able signs in the perplexing dance of romance.

The job of avian correspondence reaches out past the prompt requirements of individual birds, affecting the more extensive elements of biological systems. Birds frequently go about as natural pointers, with changes in their vocalizations or ways of behaving reflecting changes in environment wellbeing and environment conditions. Concentrating on these markers gives important bits of knowledge into the general wellbeing of environments and helps guide protection endeavors.

Innovation has turned into an important apparatus in deciphering the language of birds. Bioacoustics, the investigation of the sounds created by living creatures, permits specialists to examine and index the perplexing examples of birdsong. High level recording hardware, combined with AI calculations, empowers the distinguishing proof and following of individual bird species in light of their vocalizations. These mechanical advances improve how we might interpret avian correspondence and its job in the more extensive biological setting.

Preservation drives additionally influence innovation to screen and safeguard bird populaces. Acoustic observing, using varieties of receivers and recording gadgets, permits scientists to follow changes in bird populaces and ways of behaving over the long haul. These checking endeavors add to the ID of basic territories, the appraisal of biodiversity, and the advancement of techniques to relieve the effects of human exercises on avian networks.

7.3 Discuss the role of the atmosphere and celestial bodies in the symphonic narrative.

In the fantastic orchestra of presence, the job of the environment and divine bodies turns into an enormous suggestion that shapes the story of life on The planet. The air, a powerful envelope of gases encompassing our planet, fills in as the stage whereupon the show of climate, environment, and the breath of life unfurls. All the while, heavenly bodies — divine bodies going from the brilliant sun and the shiny moon to far off stars and planets — add divine songs to the ensemble, their gravitational dance coordinating the enormous rhythms that reverberate through the universe.

The climate, an apparently meager cover, assumes a significant part in supporting life on The planet. Made basically out of nitrogen, oxygen, and follow gases, the air fills in as a defensive safeguard, separating destructive sun powered radiation and managing temperatures. This vaporous envelope likewise turns into a mode for the musical developments of climate frameworks, environmental dissemination, and the delicate murmurs of the breeze.

The ensemble starts with the brilliant energy of the sun, the heavenly director whose iridescent implement arranges the dance of life on The planet. Sunlight based radiation, a fountain of photons spilling through the vacuum of room, experiences the World's air and changes into a heap of shades and energies. Daylight washes the planet in warmth, making way for the photosynthetic expressive dance of plants — a crucial part of the worldwide biological system.

Photosynthesis, the catalytic interaction by which plants convert daylight into compound energy, shapes the structure of the air and gives food to the bunch animals that possess the Earth. The environmental suggestion takes on a green shade as chlorophyll-bearing organic entities retain daylight, delivering oxygen high up. This oxygen turns into the breath of life for endless species, a crucial part of the orchestra that underlies the sensitive equilibrium of the biosphere.

As the sun proceeds with its heavenly excursion across the sky, the environment turns into a material painted with mists, those fleeting brushstrokes of dense water fume. Mists, in their different structures and pieces, add surface to the barometrical creation. Cumulus mists, feathery and white, summon a feeling of energy, while cirrus mists, wispy and high-elevation, follow fragile examples against the blue spread.

The developments of mists, driven by barometrical dissemination designs, make the artful dance of climate frameworks. Winds, those imperceptible artists, convey dampness loaded air masses across the globe, prompting the musical crescendos of downpour, snow, and tempests. Thunder, a percussive component in the climatic orchestra, reverberates through the air as lightning enlightens the stage, projecting a sensational presentation against the scenery of the evening.

The air's part in the water cycle further enhances the ensemble. Vanishing lifts water from seas, lakes, and streams out of sight, framing the ethereal notes of water fume. Buildup, the environmental partner to photosynthesis, changes these notes into mists, making the expectant development that goes before the arrival of precipitation. Downpour, a delicate sound or a heavy storm, turns into a fluid development in the environmental ensemble, supporting the earth underneath.

The heavenly bodies, in their everlasting dance across the enormous stage, add layers of intricacy to the musical account. The moon, Earth's sidekick, fluctuates in a heavenly expressive dance that impacts tides and enlightens the evening. The gravitational interchange among Earth and the moon, an infinite two part harmony, makes flowing developments that reverberation through the seas, further entwining the earthbound and heavenly components of the orchestra.

Past the moon, the planets of our planetary group join the heavenly tune. Every planet, with its special qualities and orbital examples, contributes its own divine tune to the ensemble.

The gas goliaths, similar to Jupiter and Saturn, with their enormous airs and glorious rings, make profound bass notes in the astronomical sythesis. The rough planets, including Earth, add their own harmonies, following circular ways around the sun in the vast dance of planetary circles.

Stars, those far off iridescent circles, enlighten the enormous span with their brilliant sparkle. The heavenly bodies, made out of interconnected stars that structure natural examples in the night sky, become divine notes in the fabulous sythesis of the universe. Old societies, enraptured by the stars' glimmering tunes, wove fantasies and legends around these heavenly creatures, changing the night sky into a divine embroidery of narrating.

Among the stars, the sun becomes the overwhelming focus as the brilliant wellspring of energy that supports life on The planet. The sun's brilliant notes, discharged in a persistent stream of sun oriented radiation, traverse the endlessness of room to arrive at our planet. These divine notes, a combination of hydrogen iotas in the sun's center, become the basic harmonies that resound through the orchestra of life on The planet.

The musical account stretches out past our nearby planet group, venturing into the profundities of the universe and the more extensive universe. Clouds, those inestimable billows of gas and residue, become the ethereal harmonies that bring forth new stars. Supernovae, touchy finales of enormous stars, discharge vast shockwaves that resonate through the interstellar medium, making dynamic developments in the astronomical ensemble.

The greatness of the universe turns out to be most obvious in the astronomical foundation radiation, the weak reverberations of the Enormous detonation that penetrate the universe. This early stage murmur, an infinite remainder from the introduction of the universe, highlights the immensity and relic of the musical story that has been unfurling for billions of years.

In our investigation of the universe, human innovation turns into an instrument in unraveling the divine orchestra. Telescopes, both earthbound and space-based, expand our tactile discernment into the profundities of room, permitting us to notice far off universes, nebulae, and inestimable peculiarities. Space tests, messengers sent off into the vast void, communicate back the reverberations of their experiences, adding another layer to the astronomical story.

The environmental orchestra, with its earthly and divine developments, turns into an impression of the interconnectedness, everything being equal. The sensitive equilibrium of the environment supports life on The planet, giving the stage whereupon the ensemble of biological systems, climate, and divine connections unfurls. Heavenly bodies, in their vast dance, contribute their divine songs, making an amicable organization that rises above the limits of our planet and reaches out into the more extensive universe.

As stewards of this fragile orchestra, humankind faces the obligation of protecting the circumstances that permit life to prosper on The planet. Environmental change, driven by human exercises, represents a danger to the barometrical equilibrium, disturbing weather conditions and increasing the musical developments of tempests and outrageous occasions. Protection endeavors, manageable practices, and a more profound comprehension of the interconnectedness of Earth and universe become fundamental notes in the continuous creation of the environmental and heavenly orchestra.

In examining the climatic and divine ensemble, there is an acknowledgment that our reality is nevertheless a passing second in the great story of the universe. The Earth, suspended in the boundlessness of room, turns into a small note in the vast score. However, inside this infinite point of view, the orchestra of life on our planet holds an interesting and valuable tune — a song that resounds through the air, across the heavenly bodies, and into the inestimable territory. As we pay attention to this musical account, may we track down motivation to appreciate and safeguard the fragile exchange of Earth and universe, perceiving the excellence and meaning of our job in the grandiose orchestra.

The orchestra of the universe, woven through the divine bodies that embellish the enormous stage, unfurls in a great story that traverses the tremendous scope of existence. Heavenly bodies, going from the brilliant sun and shimmering moon to far off stars, planets, and worlds, contribute their glowing notes to this excellent enormous organization. Their gravitational moves, brilliant discharges, and dynamic cooperations make an instrumental work of art that resounds through the universe, rising above the constraints of human comprehension.

At the core of this musical story is the sun, an inestimable illuminating presence whose brilliant energy fills in as the heavenly director organizing the dance of life on The planet. The sun, a fuming wad of superheated plasma, emanates a constant stream of photons that movement through the vacuum of room to arrive at our planet. This sun oriented radiation turns into the principal energy hotspot for life on The planet, driving photosynthesis — the catalytic interaction by which plants convert daylight into synthetic energy.

As daylight washes the Earth, it makes way for the photosynthetic expressive dance of plants — a significant demonstration in the enormous show. Chlorophyll, the green color in plant cells, retains daylight and utilizations its energy to change over carbon dioxide and water into glucose, delivering oxygen as a side-effect. This dance of particles and energy changes the World's climate and supports the many-sided trap of life. Oxygen, the breath of life, turns into a divine note in the climatic ensemble, personally associated with the sun based tunes radiating from the sun.

The moon, Earth's heavenly sidekick, adds its own iridescent notes to the ensemble. In the nighttime sky, the moon comes and goes, following its curved circle all over our world.

The gravitational interchange among Earth and the moon makes flowing developments, adding a cadenced quality to the divine organization. Tides, impacted by the moon's gravitational force, rhythmic movement in a grandiose dance that associates the earthbound and divine domains.

Past the moon, the planets of our planetary group join the divine chorale. Every planet, with its exceptional qualities and orbital examples, contributes its own heavenly song to the orchestra. The gas goliaths — Jupiter and Saturn — with their huge environments and great rings, make profound bass notes in the vast piece. The rough planets, including Earth, add harmonies that reverberate in the heavenly ensemble, following curved ways around the sun in the grandiose dance of planetary circles.

The dance of planets stretches out to the more extensive universe, where exoplanets — planets circling stars past our planetary group — add new aspects to the enormous orchestra. Cosmologists, outfitted with telescopes and high level instrumentation, distinguish the weak marks of exoplanets through techniques like the travel strategy and outspread speed estimations. These far off planets, recently concealed in the vast spread, become divine notes in the continuous investigation of the universe.

Stars, those far off iridescent circles, enlighten the vast span with their brilliant shine. The heavenly bodies, made out of interconnected stars framing natural examples in the night sky, become divine notes in the stupendous arrangement of the universe. Old societies, dazzled by the stars' sparkling tunes, wove fantasies and legends around these heavenly creatures, changing the night sky into a divine embroidery of narrating.

The magnificence of the universe turns out to be most evident in the grandiose foundation radiation, the weak reverberations of the Huge explosion that penetrate the universe. This early stage murmur, an enormous leftover from the introduction of the universe, highlights the limitlessness and relic of the musical story that has been unfurling for billions of years. Distinguished as a weak shine in the microwave part of the electromagnetic range, the enormous foundation radiation fills in as a grandiose refrain — a steady sign of the vast orchestra's profound association with the beginnings of the universe.

Clouds, those astronomical billows of gas and residue, become the ethereal harmonies that bring forth new stars. In the twirling profundities of these heavenly nurseries, gas and residue breakdown affected by gravity, framing protostars that at last light and sparkle with heavenly brightness. The birth cries of stars reverberation through the inestimable medium, making divine developments that resound through the interstellar region.

Supernovae, the unstable finales of monstrous stars, add enormous crescendos to the orchestra. At the point when a huge star depletes its atomic fuel, gravitational breakdown sets off a destructive blast, delivering a colossal eruption of energy and sending shockwaves undulating through the infinite medium. These enormous shockwaves, conveying weighty components fashioned in the core of the perishing star, become stardust that improves the interstellar climate, adding to the arrangement of new stars and planetary frameworks.

Universes, huge vast islands made out of stars, gas, and dull matter, structure the stupendous developments in the enormous ensemble. Spiraling cosmic systems, like the Smooth Way, grandstand the many-sided dance of stars inside their arms. Circular systems, with their smooth and balanced shapes, add a feeling of grandiose request to the tremendous vast embroidery. The vast orchestra stretches out to the most profound spans of room, where universe bunches and superclusters make agreeable designs on the biggest astronomical scales.

Quasars, extreme wellsprings of radiation controlled by supermassive dark openings at the focuses of worlds, transmit heavenly shouts that puncture the astronomical quietness. These far off and baffling items, found as semi heavenly radio sources, challenge how we might interpret the inestimable ensemble and the enormous cycles that oversee the way of behaving of issue and energy on grandiose scales.

In our investigation of the universe, human innovation turns into an instrument in translating the heavenly orchestra. Telescopes, both earthly and space-based, expand our tangible insight into the profundities of room, permitting us to notice far off systems, nebulae, and infinite peculiarities. Space tests, messengers sent off into the infinite void, communicate back the reverberations of their experiences, adding another layer to the astronomical account. Satellites, circling the Earth and other heavenly bodies, give significant information that advances how we might interpret the divine notes that penetrate the universe.

The musical account stretches out past our planetary group, venturing into the profundities of the world and the more extensive universe. The infinite web, an immense and interconnected organization of fibers and voids that stretches across the universe, turns into the setting for the enormous orchestra. Dull matter, a tricky and baffling inestimable part, impacts the infinite developments through its gravitational draw, adding an inconspicuous and ethereal quality to the grandiose piece.

As we dive into the grandiose ensemble, the idea of dim energy arises as a puzzling power that pushes the development of the universe. Dull energy, representing the sped up enormous development, turns into a vast contradiction that challenges how we might interpret the key powers and elements that oversee the universe. The transaction between dull matter and dim energy turns into a divine two part harmony that shapes the predetermination of the universe.

The vast orchestra, with its heavenly developments and enormous harmonies, welcomes consideration of mankind's spot in the fabulous account of the universe. The Earth, suspended in the immensity of room, turns into a little note in the enormous score. However, inside this inestimable viewpoint, the ensemble of life on our planet holds a one of a kind and valuable tune — a song that resounds through the divine bodies, across the huge infinite distances, and into the actual heart of the universe.

In pondering the divine ensemble, there is an acknowledgment that our reality is nevertheless a transient second in the great story of the universe. The heavenly bodies, with their brilliant energies and gravitational moves, become inestimable instruments that add to the continuous organization of the universe. As we pay attention to this heavenly ensemble, may we track down motivation to investigate the universe, open its secrets, and value the magnificence and intricacy of the divine story that has been unfurling for ages. In doing as such, we become enormous audience members, sensitive to the divine notes that reverberation through the huge vast scope, associating us to the glory of the universe.

Chapter 8

Crescendo of Conservation

In the steadily developing embroidery of human life, the crescendo of preservation has arisen as a resonating source of inspiration. As the ensemble of progress plays on, it turns out to be progressively obvious that our planet is a delicate song, gently made more than billions out of years. The concordance of biological systems and biodiversity is in danger of being overwhelmed by the disharmony of ecological debasement and environmental change.

The criticalness of protection has arrived at a crescendo, reverberating through the hallways of logical exploration, strategy making chambers, and grassroots developments. At its center, protection is the craftsmanship and study of safeguarding the sensitive equilibrium of nature, guaranteeing the endurance of species, environments, and at last, our own human life. The crescendo is powered by a developing familiarity with the interconnectedness of all life on The planet, where the destiny of a solitary animal groups can resonate through the whole ensemble of presence.

As the human populace thrives and industrialization floods forward, the burdens on our planet have become progressively clear. Environments once overflowing with life presently face the unpropitious danger of breakdown, as deforestation, contamination, and environmental change adjust the actual texture of the regular world. The crescendo of protection is a reaction to this hazard, an aggregate work to invert the grating notes of ecological corruption and make a reasonable tune for people in the future.

In the tremendous suggestion of preservation, biodiversity becomes the overwhelming focus. The lavishness and assortment of life on Earth are the strings that wind around together the complex embroidery of biological systems. Be that as it may, this biodiversity is under attack as human exercises infringe upon regular territories, prompting the elimination of species at a disturbing rate. The crescendo of protection looks to stem this tide, perceiving that the passing of a solitary animal groups can unwind the perplexing trap of life, making hopeless harm biological systems and the administrations they give.

The predicament of notable species, like elephants, tigers, and rhinos, catches public consideration and fills in as a mobilizing point for preservation endeavors. The crescendo ascents as moderates endeavor to safeguard these charming megafauna, perceiving their job as cornerstone species that shape the scenes they occupy. However, the ensemble of preservation reaches out past the spotlight of these lead species to embrace the innumerable unrecognized yet truly great individuals of biodiversity - the pollinators, decomposers, and bunch different living beings that structure the perplexing mosaic of life.

Safeguarded regions and untamed life holds stand as defenses against the infringement of human exercises, giving safe-havens where biodiversity can flourish. The crescendo of preservation is reflected in the foundation and development of these safeguarded regions, going from tremendous unsettled areas to metropolitan green spaces. Nonetheless, the test lies in making these shelters as well as in guaranteeing their successful administration and network to shape a durable organization that permits species to move and biological systems to adjust to evolving conditions.

Protection is definitely not a static undertaking; a powerful cycle requires persistent transformation to the developing difficulties presented by human exercises and natural changes. The crescendo resonates in the passages of examination organizations and research facilities where researchers dive into the secrets of nature, hereditary qualities, and conduct to open the mysteries of species and environments. Preservation science, a multidisciplinary field at the convergence of environment, hereditary qualities, and development, assumes a vital part in directing protection techniques.

Despite fast natural change, protection hereditary qualities arises as a pivotal instrument, offering bits of knowledge into the hereditary variety of populaces and their capacity to adjust to new circumstances.

The crescendo ascents as researchers utilize hereditary information to illuminate reproducing projects, movements, and different mediations pointed toward reinforcing the versatility of imperiled species. Simultaneously, preservation physiology gives a window into the physiological reactions of organic entities to ecological stressors, directing endeavors to moderate the effects of environmental change and different dangers.

Innovation, as well, loans its rhythm to the crescendo of protection. Remote detecting, satellite symbolism, and geographic data frameworks (GIS) empower traditionalists to screen changes in land cover, track natural life developments, and evaluate the soundness of biological systems for a huge scope. Drones rise above scenes, catching information that was once out of reach, while camera traps quietly notice subtle animals in their regular territories. The combination of innovation into protection endeavors enhances the scope and effect of drives pointed toward defending biodiversity.

Protection isn't the selective space of researchers and specialists; an aggregate undertaking connects with networks, policymakers, and people around the world. The crescendo resonates in the voices of native people groups who have been the stewards of their properties for ages, their conventional information offering important bits of knowledge into feasible asset the board. Local area based preservation drives engage neighborhood occupants to become dynamic members in the security of their normal legacy, cultivating a feeling of pride and obligation regarding the biological systems they possess.

Arrangements and regulation structure the legitimate system that supports protection endeavors, and the crescendo of preservation reverberations in the corridors of government where choices are made that can shape the destiny of environments. The foundation of safeguarded regions, the guideline of land use, and the requirement of hostile to poaching estimates the entire fall inside the domain of protection strategies. Peaceful accords, like the Show on Natural Variety, give a worldwide structure to tending to the interconnected difficulties of biodiversity misfortune, environmental change, and feasible turn of events.

Monetary instruments, including awards, sponsorships, and eco-the travel industry income, assume a basic part in supporting protection endeavors. The crescendo is enhanced by the help of magnanimous associations, administrative organizations, and naturally cognizant organizations that perceive the benefit of putting resources into the safeguarding of biodiversity. In reality as we know it where monetary interests frequently conflict with protection needs, creative supporting components, for example, installments for biological system administrations, look to adjust financial impetuses to environmental manageability.

Instruction arises as a foundation of the crescendo of preservation, as mindfulness and understanding structure the bedrock of an aggregate obligation to protecting the climate. Natural schooling programs, outreach drives, and correspondence crusades intend to motivate a feeling of ecological stewardship since the beginning.

The orchestra of preservation is advanced as people and networks become educated advocates, settling on economical decisions in their day to day routines and pushing for approaches that focus on the soundness of the planet.

The worldwide idea of natural difficulties requires cooperation and coordination on a remarkable scale. The crescendo grows as global associations, non-administrative elements, and legislatures cooperate to address transboundary issues, for example, environmental change, unlawful untamed life exchange, and the spread of intrusive species. Preservation discretion turns into a blending force, cultivating partnerships and arrangements that rise above international limits chasing shared natural objectives.

Environmental change, driven by human exercises, remains as a focal subject in the crescendo of preservation. The warming of the planet represents a significant danger to environments, changing precipitation designs, expanding the recurrence and power of outrageous climate occasions, and driving changes in the circulation of species.

Preservation methodologies should adjust to these evolving conditions, integrating environment brilliant methodologies that improve the versatility of biological systems and species.

The protection of normal living spaces is inseparably connected to the prosperity of human social orders. The crescendo reverberations in the acknowledgment that sound biological systems give a huge number of administrations fundamental for human endurance, from clean air and water to fertilization of yields and guideline of illness. Protection endeavors that focus on the safeguarding of biodiversity likewise add to the accomplishment of more extensive supportable improvement objectives, making an amicable harmony between the requirements of individuals and the strength of the planet.

The crescendo of protection faces impressive difficulties, from the tireless walk of deforestation to the unavoidable impact of contamination in air, land, and water. Obtrusive species, driven by globalization and human exercises, upset biological systems and outcompete local vegetation. Over-double-dealing of normal assets, driven by a developing worldwide populace and unreasonable utilization designs, puts extra weight on biological systems previously wrestling with the effects of environmental change.

The termination emergency, set apart by the quick and phenomenal loss of species, creates a shaded area over the crescendo of preservation. The fragile songs of nature are quieted as species disappear before they can be considered, their possible commitments to medication, farming, and environmental equilibrium lost for eternity. Protectionists attempt to beat the clock, endeavoring to forestall the eradication of species and reestablish populaces through hostage reproducing, environment rebuilding, and different mediations.

Preservation morals and reasoning imbue the crescendo with a more profound reverberation, provoking mankind to rethink its relationship with the regular world. The acknowledgment of the natural worth of every living being, no matter what their utility to people, shapes the underpinning of a moral system that rises above anthropocentrism. Protection becomes a logical need as well as an ethical goal, pull in a worship forever and an acknowledgment of our common obligation as stewards of the Earth.

The crescendo of preservation reaches out past the earthly domain to embrace the seas, where marine environments face a horde of dangers, from overfishing and living space obliteration to plastic contamination and sea fermentation. The orchestra reverberates in the endeavors to lay out marine safeguarded regions, direct fishing rehearses, and moderate the effects of environmental change on coral reefs and other weak biological systems. The soundness of the seas is unpredictably connected to the prosperity of the whole planet, and the crescendo of preservation looks to guarantee the essentialness of these watery domains.

As the crescendo of preservation resonates across the globe, it experiences the intricacies of human way of behaving and cultural qualities. The quest for financial development frequently clashes with protection needs, prompting tough decisions and compromises. The ensemble faces the test of rousing a change in social perspectives, cultivating a more profound association among individuals and the regular world. Preservation correspondence turns into a craftsmanship, winding around stories that resound with different crowds and move an aggregate obligation to maintainable living.

The job of native information and customary environmental insight adds a rich layer to the crescendo of preservation. Native people groups, who have supported themselves as one with nature for centuries, offer significant bits of knowledge into feasible land the executives, asset preservation, and the complex connections among people and the climate. The orchestra is enhanced as customary information is coordinated into current preservation procedures, making a more comprehensive and socially delicate way to deal with natural stewardship.

The crescendo of preservation reverberates in the security of existing biodiversity as well as in the rebuilding of corrupted biological systems. Protectionists and rebuilding environmentalists work connected at the hip to restore scenes that have been changed by human exercises, from debased backwoods and wetlands to metropolitan green spaces. Biological reclamation turns into a critical instrument in the ensemble, offering expect the recuperation of environments and the species that rely upon them.

The force of joint effort enhances the crescendo of preservation, as different partners meet up in quest for a shared objective. Protection associations between legislatures, non-administrative associations, neighborhood networks, and the confidential area tackle aggregate skill and assets to address complex difficulties. The ensemble acquires strength as collusions structure across areas, making a unified front against the powers of natural corruption.

Amidst the crescendo, the significance of youth commitment arises as a groundbreaking power. The more youthful age, acquiring the tradition of past ecological choices, ventures onto the stage intensely for supportability and an assurance to shape a more agreeable future. Youth-drove developments, natural instruction programs, and the mix of youth voices into dynamic cycles add to the liveliness of the orchestra of preservation.

The crescendo of preservation arrives at its apex in the acknowledgment that humankind is a basic piece of the regular world, interconnected with each living being and woven into the many-sided texture of environments. Protection turns into an excursion of self-revelation, an acknowledgment that the prosperity of the planet is indistinguishable from our own. The ensemble welcomes us to tune in, to comprehend, and to act working together with the rhythms of nature.

In the last developments of the crescendo, the center goes to what's to come. The ensemble of preservation imagines an existence where mankind resides together as one with the planet, where the variety of life twists, and environments flourish. Economical practices, protection strategies, and moral standards guide the way ahead, guaranteeing that the crescendo doesn't disappear yet keeps on resounding through the ages to come.

In the calm consequence of the crescendo, the reverberations wait, helping us to remember our aggregate liability to sustain and safeguard the valuable orchestra of life. The excursion of protection is progressing, a dynamic and developing cycle that requires commitment, development, and an agreeable coordinated effort among humankind and the regular world. The crescendo of protection welcomes us to become dynamic members in this fantastic ensemble, each assuming a novel part in the safeguarding of the fragile tunes that wind around together the embroidery of life on The planet.

8.1 Examine the current state of environmental conservation efforts globally.

The present status of natural preservation endeavors universally mirrors a complicated embroidery of progress, challenges, and the earnest requirement for aggregate activity. Against the background of heightening ecological emergencies, including environmental change, biodiversity misfortune, and natural surroundings debasement, the crescendo of protection resounds as mankind wrestles with the basic to shield the planet for people in the future.

Vital to the assessment of the worldwide protection scene is the affirmation that we are at a basic point. The impacts of environmental change are turning out to be progressively clear, with increasing worldwide temperatures, more incessant and serious outrageous climate occasions, and interruptions to biological systems. Biodiversity, the unpredictable trap of life that supports environments and offers fundamental types of assistance, faces uncommon dangers as human exercises keep on adjusting normal territories, drive species to elimination, and compromise the versatility of whole biological systems.

At the core of protection endeavors is the acknowledgment that these difficulties are interconnected. Environmental change, for example, fuels existing tensions on biodiversity, while the deficiency of biodiversity, thusly, debilitates biological systems' capacity to relieve and adjust to environmental change. The desperation of resolving these interlaced issues is highlighted by the logical agreement that mankind has entered another land age, the Anthropocene, described by the significant impact of human exercises on the World's frameworks.

Protection endeavors at the worldwide level are moored in peaceful accords and structures that try to address the underlying drivers of ecological debasement. The Paris Understanding, embraced in 2015, addresses a milestone responsibility by countries to restrict an unnatural weather change to well under 2 degrees Celsius above pre-modern levels. In any case, the difficulties lie in setting aggressive focuses as well as in making an interpretation of these responsibilities into unmistakable activities that lead to outflows decreases and manageable turn of events.

One of the basic parts of looking at worldwide preservation endeavors is the job of biodiversity protection. The Show on Organic Variety (CBD), a thorough worldwide settlement, fills in as the foundation for worldwide endeavors to ration and economically use biodiversity. The Aichi Biodiversity Targets, embraced under the CBD, put forth essential objectives to address biodiversity misfortune by 2020. As the objective year passed, a sobering reflection uncovers that the majority of these objectives were not met, highlighting the criticalness of intensifying endeavors to secure and reestablish biodiversity.

Safeguarded regions, fundamental for protecting biodiversity and keeping up with biological system administrations, are necessary to worldwide preservation methodologies. Be that as it may, the viability of these areas is dependent upon sufficient subsidizing, hearty administration, and thought of the requirements and privileges of neighborhood networks. The worldwide local area faces the test of extending the inclusion of safeguarded regions as well as guaranteeing their availability, versatility, and ability to adjust to changing ecological circumstances.

The multifaceted dance among protection and reasonable improvement becomes the dominant focal point in the assessment of worldwide endeavors. The 2030 Plan for Manageable Turn of events, with its 17 Feasible Advancement Objectives (SDGs), perceives the interlinkages between natural, social, and monetary aspects. While SDG 15 expressly centers around life ashore and biodiversity protection, the progress of all objectives relies upon a sound and tough planet. The strain between improvement goals and protection objectives requires imaginative methodologies that accommodate human necessities with biological manageability.

In the domain of environmental change moderation, the worldwide local area is wrestling with the basic to progress to a low-carbon economy. The reception of sustainable power sources, energy proficiency measures, and the progressively eliminating of petroleum products are basic parts of this change. The Paris Understanding's objective of accomplishing a harmony between anthropogenic discharges and evacuations of ozone depleting substances in the last part of this century highlights the requirement for extraordinary changes in energy, industry, and land use.

Be that as it may, the change to a manageable future faces various difficulties. Financial interests, political contemplations, and dug in frameworks present obstructions to the fast and broad reception of feasible practices. The assessment of worldwide protection endeavors uncovers a requirement for strategy rationality that coordinates ecological contemplations into dynamic cycles across areas. The organization of market components, for example, carbon evaluating, can boost emanations decreases and furnish financial signs that line up with preservation objectives.

The job of innovation in worldwide preservation endeavors is a situation with two sides. On one hand, mechanical headways offer instruments for observing ecological changes, breaking down information, and illuminating preservation procedures. Satellite symbolism, remote detecting, and AI add to how we might interpret environments and empower more designated intercessions. Then again, innovation additionally supports a significant number of the exercises driving ecological corruption, from deforestation to overfishing. Finding some kind of harmony that saddles the positive capability of innovation while relieving its adverse consequences is a basic part of the worldwide protection plan.

Worldwide preservation endeavors can't be separated from the social components of natural difficulties. Native people groups and neighborhood networks, who frequently endure the worst part of natural debasement, assume a pivotal part in protection. The acknowledgment of their freedoms, conventional information, and dynamic cooperation in dynamic cycles are fundamental for the outcome of protection drives. Comprehensive preservation moves toward that consider the necessities and viewpoints of different partners add to the supportability and authenticity of worldwide endeavors.

The assessment of the present status of worldwide protection endeavors should likewise wrestle with the diligent issue of ecological equity. Weak people group, excessively impacted by ecological risks, face a horde of difficulties, from absence of admittance to clean water and air to the effects of environment prompted uprooting. The worldwide preservation plan should focus on value, guaranteeing that the advantages of protection don't build exclusively to favored bunches while weak networks bear the expenses.

Finance arises as a basic empowering agent and limitation in the domain of worldwide preservation endeavors. Sufficient subsidizing is fundamental for the foundation and the board of safeguarded regions, execution of protection activities, and backing for feasible advancement drives.

The Worldwide Climate Office (GEF) and the Green Environment Asset (GCF) are among the monetary systems intended to channel assets towards ecological protection and environment activity. Notwithstanding, the supporting hole stays a huge test, with the requirement for expanded ventures and inventive subsidizing components that influence public and confidential assets.

The assessment of worldwide preservation endeavors uncovers a change in outlook towards perceiving the worth of nature past its instrumental advantages. The idea of environment administrations, including the substantial and elusive commitments of biological systems to human prosperity, has acquired unmistakable quality. From the arrangement of clean water and fertilization of yields to social and sporting qualities, biological systems are necessary to human social orders. The shift towards a more comprehensive comprehension of the worth of nature highlights the requirement for protection methodologies that go past a tight spotlight on biodiversity and embrace the more extensive setting of biological system working.

The ascent of resident science and local area based checking intensifies the range and effect of worldwide protection endeavors. Conventional residents, equipped with cell phones and an energy for the climate, contribute important information that improve how we might interpret species conveyance, screen natural changes, and consider specialists responsible. The democratization of information assortment engages people and networks to partake in preservation, encouraging a feeling of pride and obligation regarding the normal world effectively.

The viability of worldwide protection endeavors is characteristically connected to administration designs and global participation. The assessment uncovers the requirement for reinforced organizations, upgraded straightforwardness, and further developed authorization of natural guidelines. Multilateral coordinated efforts, for example, the Intergovernmental Science-Strategy Stage on Biodiversity and Biological system Administrations (IPBES), give a stage to incorporating logical information and illuminating arrangement choices. In any case, the viability of these coordinated efforts depends on political will, responsibility, and a common perspective of the desperation of worldwide protection challenges.

The continuous assessment of worldwide protection endeavors highlights the significance of versatile administration. Preservation systems should develop because of new data, changing natural circumstances, and examples gained from past drives. Adaptability, flexibility, and an eagerness to gain from the two victories and disappointments are fundamental credits of successful protection programs. The idea of "working back better" after ecological emergencies accentuates the open door to reestablish biological systems as well as address the main drivers of natural corruption.

All in all, the present status of worldwide protection endeavors illustrates both advancement and squeezing difficulties. The earnestness of tending to environmental change, biodiversity misfortune, and other ecological issues requires an organized and supported exertion at the worldwide, country.

8.2 Discuss success stories and challenges in preserving biodiversity.

The safeguarding of biodiversity is a perplexing and multi-layered try that includes a horde of partners, from neighborhood networks to worldwide associations. As we dive into the conversation of examples of overcoming adversity and difficulties in saving biodiversity, it is essential to recognize the interconnectedness of the planet's environments and the significant ramifications of biodiversity misfortune on the prosperity of both normal frameworks and human social orders.

Examples of overcoming adversity in biodiversity protection frequently rise up out of purposeful endeavors to address explicit dangers to biological systems and species. One prominent model is the recuperation of the bald eagle (Haliaeetus leucocephalus) in the US. Once wavering near the precarious edge of elimination because of the far and wide utilization of the pesticide DDT, which caused eggshell diminishing and regenerative disappointment, the bald eagle has gotten back in the saddle. The prohibiting of DDT in the mid 1970s, combined with living space security measures and serious protection endeavors, has prompted a huge expansion in bald eagle populaces. The expulsion of the species from the imperiled species list in 2007 denoted a victory in the continuous fight for avian protection.

Another example of overcoming adversity unfurls in the rainforests of Costa Rica, where creative preservation methodologies have added to the security of biodiversity while cultivating feasible turn of events. Costa Rica's Installment for Environment Administrations (PES) program remains as a spearheading drive that monetarily repays landowners for safeguarding and reestablishing woods. By relegating a substantial monetary worth to the environment administrations given by backwoods, for example, carbon sequestration and watershed security, the PES program boosts landowners to take part in protection rehearses. Costa Rica's obligation to reforestation and the foundation of safeguarded regions has brought about the recovery of natural surroundings and the recuperation of species, displaying the potential for orchestrating protection and human prosperity.

Moreover, people group based protection drives have exhibited their viability in saving biodiversity while engaging nearby occupants. The Namibian government's shared conservancy program gives an enlightening model. Despite raising human-natural life clashes and dangers to untamed life populaces, the program awards neighborhood networks the freedoms to oversee and profit from untamed life on their territories. This approach has decreased struggle among people and untamed life as well as given financial motivations to networks to participate in protection.

Victories incorporate the recuperation of populaces of dark rhinoceros and the protection of cheetahs, exhibiting the potential for cooperative methodologies that coordinate the necessities of neighborhood networks with preservation targets.

Nonetheless, in the midst of these examples of overcoming adversity, a heap of difficulties endure, creating a shaded area over worldwide biodiversity protection endeavors. One of the most inescapable dangers is territory misfortune and discontinuity, driven basically by horticultural extension, urbanization, and foundation improvement. The continuous transformation of normal environments into croplands, field, and metropolitan regions disturbs biological systems, decreases accessible natural surroundings for species, and sections scenes. The outcomes are desperate, with species confronting expanded weakness to predation, decreased admittance to assets, and limited relocation pathways. Tending to the test of natural surroundings misfortune requires a fragile harmony between human turn of events and the safeguarding of basic environments.

Intrusive species represent a considerable deterrent to biodiversity conservation, frequently outcompeting local greenery and upsetting biological equilibrium. The presentation of non-local species through human exercises, like worldwide exchange and travel, has prompted the multiplication of intrusive plants, creatures, and microbes. The effect of obtrusive species is especially articulated on islands, where remarkable environments advanced in disconnection and are more defenseless to outside impacts. The annihilation or control of intrusive species requests facilitated worldwide endeavors, severe biosecurity measures, and imaginative procedures to reestablish biological systems impacted by attacks.

The overexploitation of regular assets represents a grave danger to biodiversity, especially for species focused on for exchange, hunting, or gathering. Impractical fishing rehearses, driven by expanding worldwide interest for fish, have demolished marine populaces and upset marine environments. Likewise, the unlawful natural life exchange, filled by interest for extraordinary pets, conventional medication, and extravagance products, puts monstrous strain on species like elephants, rhinos, and pangolins. The test lies not just in authorizing guidelines and fighting criminal operations yet in addition in advancing supportable other options and changing customer ways of behaving.

Environmental change arises as an inescapable and overall test that mixtures existing dangers to biodiversity. The climb in worldwide temperatures, modified precipitation designs, and the recurrence of outrageous climate occasions present uncommon difficulties to environments and species. Numerous species face the predicament of adjusting to quickly evolving conditions, relocating to additional reasonable territories, or confronting the gamble of termination. Environmental change compounds existing stressors, like natural surroundings misfortune and sickness, and requires versatile administration systems that expect and answer the biological effects of an evolving environment.

In the domain of marine preservation, coral reefs stand as both notable biological systems and signs of natural wellbeing. The dying of coral reefs, a peculiarity driven by raised ocean temperatures and exacerbated by environmental change, represents a serious danger to marine biodiversity. Examples of overcoming adversity in coral reef preservation include the foundation of marine safeguarded regions, feasible fishing practices, and local area commitment in reef the executives. Nonetheless, the worldwide test endures as coral reefs keep on confronting exceptional pressure, requiring earnest and facilitated activity to relieve environmental change and upgrade the versatility of these delicate biological systems.

One of the overall difficulties in saving biodiversity lies in the separation between protection endeavors and more extensive cultural qualities and monetary frameworks. The inherent worth of biodiversity frequently rivals momentary monetary interests, prompting an absence of political will, deficient subsidizing, and lacking implementation of preservation measures. The commodification of nature, where biological systems and species are seen basically as assets to take advantage of, subverts protection drives and propagates impractical practices. Tending to this challenge requires a change in outlook that perceives the intrinsic worth of biodiversity, coordinates natural contemplations into financial navigation, and cultivates a feeling of obligation and stewardship for the planet.

The job of native people groups in biodiversity safeguarding, while frequently recognized as essential, faces continuous difficulties connected with land privileges, social independence, and acknowledgment of customary information. Numerous native networks are on the cutting edges of protection endeavors, filling in as the caretakers of biodiverse districts and utilizing conventional environmental information to reasonably oversee regular assets. However, the infringement of outer powers, like extractive ventures and land advancement, undermines both the biological systems and the social respectability of native networks. Perceiving and regarding the freedoms of native people groups, guaranteeing their dynamic support in protection drives, and integrating customary information into standard protection rehearses are basic strides toward more comprehensive and powerful biodiversity safeguarding.

The hole in subsidizing for protection endeavors stays a significant test, upsetting the execution of complete and supported drives. While different worldwide assets and drives exist, the extent of monetary assets expected to address worldwide biodiversity challenges far surpasses current speculations. The lopsidedness between financing for preservation and sponsorships that help exercises adding to biodiversity misfortune, like modern farming and petroleum product extraction, highlights the requirement for a reconsideration of monetary needs. Furthermore, imaginative supporting instruments, public-private associations, and expanded humanitarian commitment can add to shutting the subsidizing hole and supporting long haul protection procedures.

The viability of preservation arrangements and drives is dependent upon hearty administration structures, straightforward dynamic cycles, and sufficient requirement systems. As a rule, feeble administration, debasement, and absence of political will sabotage preservation endeavors. The test lies in encouraging great administration at nearby, public, and worldwide levels, guaranteeing that strategies are educated by logical proof, receptive to neighborhood settings, and lined up with more extensive manageable improvement objectives. Fortifying law and order, engaging nearby networks, and cultivating responsibility are fundamental parts of tending to administration challenges in biodiversity protection.

Schooling and public mindfulness address basic parts in the worldwide work to safeguard biodiversity. While progress has been made in bringing issues to light about the significance of biodiversity and the dangers it faces, there is still a lot of work to be finished. The distinction between logical information and public getting it, combined with contending needs in schooling, obstructs the development of a far reaching protection ethic. Compelling correspondence techniques, ecological training projects, and public commitment drives are fundamental for overcome this issue.

8.3 Encourage readers to actively participate in conservation and sustainable practices.

Empowering perusers to effectively partake in preservation and embrace manageable practices is a source of inspiration that rises above individual activities to shape an additional economical and agreeable future by and large. The direness of tending to natural difficulties, from environmental change to biodiversity misfortune, requires a common obligation to dependable stewardship of the planet. By participating in smart and deliberate activities, people can become specialists of positive change, adding to the more extensive worldwide work to make an additional economical and versatile world.

At the center of this source of inspiration is the acknowledgment that singular decisions, regardless of how little, all in all fundamentally affect the climate. Straightforward way of life changes, like diminishing energy utilization, limiting waste, and settling on practical buyer decisions, can all things considered add to a more supportable and eco-accommodating world. It starts with a consciousness of the natural impression of our everyday exercises and a pledge to settling on decisions that line up with environmental prosperity.

Quite possibly of the most effective way people can partake in protection is by embracing supportable practices in their homes. Energy productivity, for example, can be accomplished through basic measures, for example, utilizing energy-proficient machines, switching out lights and gadgets when not being used, and enhancing warming and cooling frameworks. Also, lessening water utilization through careful use and taking on water-saving advances adds to the protection of this valuable asset. Supportable arranging rehearses, for example, local plant cultivating and water-wise finishing, further upgrade the ecological maintainability of individual families.

Squander decrease is another key region where people can effectively take part in preservation endeavors. Embracing the standards of lessen, reuse, and reuse limits the natural effect of waste age. This can include decreasing single-utilize plastic utilization, reusing materials, and reusing things to broaden their life expectancy. The reception of treating the soil rehearses further redirects natural waste from landfills, improving the dirt and decreasing ozone harming substance discharges related with squander decay.

The food decisions people make likewise assume a critical part in preservation endeavors. Embracing a plant-based or flexitarian diet has been perceived as a viable method for lessening the ecological effect related with meat creation. Animals cultivating is a significant supporter of deforestation, ozone harming substance discharges, and water contamination. By picking feasible and morally obtained food items, people can add to the protection of biological systems, support nearby ranchers, and advance horticultural practices that focus on ecological maintainability.

Transportation is a huge supporter of fossil fuel byproducts, and people can effectively partake in protection by embracing more practical methods of transportation. Picking public transportation, carpooling, trekking, or strolling diminishes fossil fuel byproducts as well as advances a better and more dynamic way of life. Moreover, the progress to electric vehicles or crossover vehicles addresses a practical decision that lines up with endeavors to moderate the effects of environmental change.

Past individual activities at home, dynamic cooperation in preservation reaches out to local area commitment and promotion. Joining nearby natural gatherings, taking part in local area tidy up occasions, and supporting protection drives enhance the effect of individual endeavors. By cultivating a feeling of local area and shared liability, people add to the making of versatile and economical networks that focus on natural prosperity.

Instructive drives and mindfulness crusades are useful assets to motivate people to take part in preservation effectively. Advancing ecological proficiency and bringing issues to light about the interconnectedness of human exercises and the wellbeing of the planet develops a feeling of obligation and strengthening. Schools, people group associations, and online stages can assume a pivotal part in dispersing data and encouraging a culture of ecological stewardship.

The advanced age offers special open doors for people to participate in preservation through innovation and online stages. Virtual entertainment can be a useful asset for sharing data, bringing issues to light, and preparing networks for natural causes. Online discussions, sites, and instructive sites give an abundance of assets to people looking for data and direction on maintainable practices. Embracing innovation additionally considers distant support in worldwide preservation drives, empowering people to add to ventures and missions no matter what their geographic area.

Supporting maintainable organizations and items is another significant way people can effectively take part in protection. By picking items with eco-accommodating certificates, supporting organizations with straightforward and maintainable practices, and inclining toward privately obtained products, people can impact market elements and advance a shift towards more reasonable and moral strategic policies. This buyer driven approach sends an unmistakable message to enterprises that focus on natural obligation.

Monetary choices likewise present open doors for people to adjust their qualities to protection endeavors. Putting resources into earth dependable assets, stripping from ventures with a huge natural effect, and supporting moral financial practices add to the redirection of monetary assets towards reasonable drives. Monetary decisions can impact corporate way of behaving and add to the development of ventures that focus on ecological maintainability.

Dynamic cooperation in preservation likewise includes pushing for approaches that help natural assurance and maintainability. Drawing in with policymakers, partaking in open meetings, and supporting regulation that tends to natural difficulties are fundamental parts of backing. People can use their aggregate voices to impact dynamic cycles and request approaches that focus on protection, environmentally friendly power, and reasonable turn of events.

The force of individual activities is amplified when joined with aggregate endeavors and a common vision for a manageable future. Worldwide developments, for example, the Fridays for Future environment strikes started by youth activists, epitomize the effect of aggregate activity in bringing issues to light and impacting strategy choices. By partaking in or supporting such developments, people add to a more extensive cultural shift towards focusing on ecological maintainability.

Volunteerism is a substantial and involved way for people to partake in protection drives effectively. Neighborhood natural associations, untamed life safe-havens, and preservation projects frequently depend on the help of workers to complete fundamental undertakings, for example, living space reclamation, natural life observing, and local area outreach. Chipping in not just gives people direct contribution in preservation endeavors yet in addition encourages a feeling of association with nature and a local area of similar people.

Training and mindfulness crusades that feature the advantages of protection and maintainable practices are urgent in motivating conduct change. Legislatures, non-legislative associations, and instructive organizations can assume a urgent part in spreading data, advancing ecological education, and encouraging a culture of manageability. Public mindfulness missions can resolve explicit issues, like plastic contamination, deforestation, or environmental change, and engage people with the information and instruments to pursue informed choices.

All in all, uplifting perusers to effectively take part in protection and embrace reasonable practices is an encouragement to be specialists of positive change despite ecological difficulties. The force of individual activities, when increased across networks and countries, can possibly make an extraordinary effect on the soundness of the planet. By pursuing informed decisions, participating in local area drives, supporting practical organizations, and upholding for strategies that focus on protection, people add to an aggregate exertion that rises above lines and ages. The source of inspiration is an affirmation of the interconnectedness of all life on The planet and an acknowledgment of the common obligation to safeguard and safeguard the magnificence and variety of the normal world for current and people in the future.

Preservation and manageable practices are at the front of tending to the pressing natural difficulties confronting our planet. The entwined issues of environmental change, biodiversity misfortune, living space debasement, and asset exhaustion require a central change by they way we communicate with the regular world. Embracing protection and manageable practices isn't just an obligation however an aggregate basic for defending the wellbeing of biological systems, advancing biodiversity, and guaranteeing an economical future for a long time into the future.

At its center, protection is the security, safeguarding, and supportable utilization of normal assets and environments. It includes a great many exercises pointed toward keeping up with and reestablishing the equilibrium of environmental frameworks, forestalling the elimination of species, and advancing the general wellbeing of the planet. Economical practices, then again, include deciding and taking on ways of behaving that adversely affect the climate, guaranteeing the capable utilization of assets to address recent concerns without compromising the capacity of people in the future to address their own issues.

The significance of preservation and maintainable practices is highlighted by the significant interconnectedness of every living being and the biological systems they occupy. Human exercises, from industrialization to farming, have essentially modified the World's normal frameworks, prompting boundless ecological debasement. The results, for example, environmental change and the deficiency of biodiversity, affect biological systems, weather conditions, and the prosperity of both human and non-human occupants of the planet.

Environmental change, driven by the aggregation of ozone harming substances in the air, is one of the most squeezing difficulties within recent memory. Protection endeavors assume an essential part in moderating environmental change by saving carbon sinks, for example, timberlands and wetlands, which sequester carbon dioxide and assist with managing the World's environment. Also, economical works on, including the progress to environmentally friendly power sources and energy productivity measures, add to lessening the discharges that drive environmental change.

Biodiversity, the assortment of life on The planet, is a proportion of the wellbeing and versatility of biological systems. Preservation is foremost in protecting biodiversity, as the deficiency of species and natural surroundings upsets biological equilibrium and reduces the limit of biological systems to adjust to ecological changes. Supportable practices, for example, capable land use and fishing rehearses, are fundamental for keeping up with sound environments and forestalling the overexploitation of species.

Environment debasement, frequently determined by deforestation, urbanization, and modern exercises, represents a critical danger to biodiversity. Preservation endeavors center around safeguarding and reestablishing environments, making untamed life halls, and laying out safeguarded regions to guarantee the endurance of assorted species. Manageable practices include land-use arranging that limits the effect on normal territories and advances conjunction between human exercises and natural life.

Asset consumption, including the over-extraction of water, deforestation, and the exhaustion of fisheries, is a result of unreasonable practices. Preservation drives look to oversee assets capably, guaranteeing their recharging and forestalling exhaustion. Supportable practices in agribusiness, ranger service, and fisheries focus on long haul asset the board, limiting waste and ecological effect.

Water protection is a basic part of feasible practices, given the fundamental job of water in supporting life. Preservation endeavors include effective water use, assurance of watersheds, and the avoidance of contamination to guarantee the accessibility of clean water for biological systems and networks. Economical water the executives rehearses incorporate water collecting, wastewater treatment, and the rebuilding of regular water cycles.

Economical agribusiness is basic to both food security and ecological preservation. Customary modern farming works on, including monoculture and extreme utilization of compound data sources, can prompt soil debasement, loss of biodiversity, and contamination. Protection disapproved of horticultural practices, for example, agroecology and regenerative cultivating, focus on soil wellbeing, biodiversity, and the utilization of natural and feasible cultivating techniques. These methodologies expect to create food in manners that are naturally mindful, monetarily reasonable, and socially fair.

The seas, covering over 70% of the World's surface, are vital to worldwide environments and environment guideline. Impractical fishing rehearses, plastic contamination, and sea fermentation are significant dangers to marine conditions. Preservation endeavors incorporate the foundation of marine safeguarded regions, maintainable fisheries the executives, and drives to diminish marine contamination. Manageable practices include dependable fish utilization, squander decrease, and supporting arrangements that safeguard marine environments.

Sustainable power sources, for example, sunlight based, wind, and hydropower, are essential in progressing away from petroleum products and alleviating environmental change. Preservation endeavors incorporate safeguarding regular regions that act as likely destinations for sustainable power projects and limiting the natural effect of energy framework. Maintainable practices include embracing and advancing clean energy innovations, further developing energy effectiveness, and upholding for strategies that help the change to a low-carbon economy.

Urbanization, while vital for obliging a developing worldwide populace, frequently brings about territory misfortune, air and water contamination, and expanded energy utilization. Protection in metropolitan regions centers around green foundation, metropolitan arranging that focuses on biodiversity, and the conservation of green spaces. Manageable metropolitan practices incorporate energy-productive structures, squander decrease, public transportation, and the coordination of nature into metropolitan plan.

Schooling and mindfulness are instrumental in cultivating a culture of protection and manageability. People assume an imperative part in driving change through informed decisions and pushing for reasonable practices in their networks. Protection schooling programs, natural missions, and drives that advance eco-proficiency engage people to comprehend the effect of their activities and pursue informed choices that add to a more practical future.

The idea of "lessen, reuse, reuse" typifies reasonable practices that people can integrate into their regular routines. Diminishing utilization, limiting waste, and picking items with insignificant ecological effect are key parts of a practical way of life. Reusing things, reusing materials, and reusing add to the round economy, where assets are utilized proficiently, and squander is limited.

Green innovations and development assume a significant part in propelling protection and reasonable practices. From eco-accommodating structure materials to progressions in sustainable power and feasible horticulture, mechanical arrangements add to limiting natural effect. Preservation advancements, like remote detecting and checking gadgets, help in untamed life protection and natural surroundings the board. Embracing and supporting these advancements is fundamental for tending to ecological difficulties.

Nearby people group commitment is a foundation of fruitful protection and maintainable practices. Networks are in many cases the stewards of regular assets and biological systems, and their association is crucial for the outcome of protection drives. Maintainable advancement projects that line up with nearby requirements, regard native information, and engage networks monetarily add to both natural and social supportability.

Corporate obligation and supportable strategic policies assume a critical part in molding a more manageable world. Organizations can add to protection endeavors by embracing harmless to the ecosystem works on, lessening their carbon impression, and integrating maintainability into their inventory chains. Accreditation programs, like natural and fair exchange, furnish shoppers with data about the ecological and social obligation of items and administrations.

Government strategies and global collaboration are fundamental for establishing an empowering climate for protection and manageable practices. Regulation that safeguards normal natural surroundings, controls asset use, and boosts reasonable practices is basic. Peaceful accords, for example, the Paris Settlement on environmental change and the Show on Natural Variety, give systems to worldwide participation in tending to ecological difficulties. Promotion for solid ecological arrangements and considering states responsible for their responsibilities are pivotal parts of the preservation plan.

Monetary motivators and ventures are amazing assets for advancing preservation and manageability. Legislatures, organizations, and people can designate assets to help preservation projects, supportable drives, and examination on inventive arrangements. Monetary organizations can assume a part by integrating ecological standards into speculation choices and supporting undertakings that decidedly affect biodiversity and environments.

Cooperation and associations among different partners are instrumental in enhancing the effect of preservation and maintainable practices. Legislatures, non-administrative associations, organizations, the scholarly world, and nearby networks can cooperate to address complex ecological difficulties. Cross-sectoral coordinated efforts influence the extraordinary qualities of every partner, prompting more far reaching and successful arrangements.

Chapter 9

Coda - A Call to Action

In the immense territory of mankind's set of experiences, ages have unfurled, each making a permanent imprint on the embroidery of presence. From the early stage battles of endurance to the perplexing dance of civic establishments, the account of mankind has been woven with strings of win and affliction. As we stand on the cliff of another period, the reverberations of our past resonate through the passageways of time, encouraging us to examine our direction and consider the inheritance we will hand down to the ages yet unborn.

In the orchestra of progress, conflicting notes frequently go with the agreeable harmonies of headway. The contemporary period is no special case, as the world wrestles with a horde of difficulties that request aggregate thoughtfulness and definitive activity. From ecological corruption to social disparity, the kaleidoscope of issues requires a bound together reaction grounded in sympathy, foreknowledge, and a steadfast obligation to a common future.

At the core of this source of inspiration lies the basic to address the environmental emergencies that undermine the actual food of life on The planet.

The tireless abuse of normal assets and the reckless negligence for the fragile equilibrium of environments have introduced a period of environmental change and biodiversity misfortune. The results are manifest in rising ocean levels, outrageous climate occasions, and the eradication of endless species. Despite such environmental disturbance, a significant reexamination of our relationship with the planet isn't just fitting yet basic.

The direness of this ecological retribution reaches out past public boundaries, rising above political and philosophical partitions. In the interconnected trap of our globalized world, the activities of one country resonate across landmasses. Consequently, an aggregate obligation to supportable practices, sustainable power sources, and protection endeavors turns into the key part of a strong and amicable future. The Coda of our period should reverberate with the songs of natural stewardship, repeating a guarantee to giving a livable planet to the approaching ages.

However, the difficulties we face reach out past the natural domain. In the mind boggling mosaic of human culture, separation points of unfairness and imbalance persevere. The gaps that different the favored from the minimized interest our consideration and a coordinated work to connect them. Separation in view of race, orientation, financial status, and other social identifiers subverts the actual texture of our common mankind.

To manufacture a more impartial world, the Coda entices us to defy fundamental treacheries and destroy the designs that propagate disparity. This requires regulative changes as well as a change in cultural cognizance — one that perceives the intrinsic pride and worth of each and every person. The quest for equity should be unrelenting, for it is in the cauldron of value that the genuine grit of a civilization is tried.

Training, as well, arises as a vital instrument in this ensemble of progress. The Coda welcomes us to rethink instruction as a groundbreaking power, separating hindrances and encouraging a feeling of request and decisive reasoning. A general public that puts resources into the scholarly strengthening of its residents develops the seeds of progress and development. In the hug of information, biases shrivel, and the opportunities for a more illuminated future expand.

As we explore the intricacies of the cutting edge age, innovation remains as both a reference point of commitment and a situation with two sides. The fast progression of man-made consciousness, biotechnology, and other outskirts sciences opens new vistas of plausibility. However, it likewise raises moral binds and moves our ability to dependably use these devices. The Coda begs us to move toward mechanical advancement with an insightful eye, guaranteeing that development serves the aggregate great as opposed to planting the seeds of strife and oppressed world.

In the midst of the tumult of our times, the domain of international relations expects a focal job in forming the fate of countries. The Coda resonates with a supplication for tact, collaboration, and the quest for shared belief.

In a period set apart by international strains and the apparition of contention, the basic of exchange and understanding turns into even more articulated. The world, it appears, has turned into a worldwide town where the destinies of countries are interwoven, and neutrality is an extravagance we can sick manage.

In diagramming a course forward, the Coda entices pioneers to transcend the limited bounds of public interests and embrace a dream that rises above borders. The difficulties within recent memory — from pandemics to monetary precariousness — require a cooperative and facilitated reaction. The establishments that oversee our reality should develop to mirror the interconnected idea of our difficulties, cultivating a feeling of fortitude that perceives our common predetermination.

Indispensable to the Coda is the acknowledgment of the extraordinary force of sympathy and compassion. During a time described by fast change and vulnerability, it is not difficult to capitulate to the troublesome powers that look to plant dissension and doubt. However, the pith of our common humankind lies in our ability to identify with the battles and yearnings of others. The Coda entreats us to develop empathy as a core value, perceiving that in the embroidery of presence, each string is joined, and the thriving of one adds to the prosperity of all.

Chasing after this amazing orchestra, the job of people becomes fundamental. Every individual, similar to a performer in an ensemble, contributes their extraordinary notes to the creation of society. The Coda welcomes us to perceive the organization innate in our activities, asking us to be aware of the effect we have on the world and its occupants. From our decisions as shoppers to the qualities we champion in our networks, the ability to shape a superior world lies in the possession of the system "we."

The excursion toward a more promising time to come requests versatility even with difficulty and a guarantee to gaining from our mix-ups. The Coda is a call to reflection, requesting that we defy our inadequacies with modesty and to see misfortunes as any open doors for development. It recognizes that the street to advance is full of difficulties, however it is in the cauldron of these difficulties that the personality of people and social orders is fashioned.

In the fantastic story of human life, the Coda isn't a determination however a progress — a scaffold between the present and what's to come. A source of inspiration reverberates across existence, encouraging us to be draftsmen of our predetermination as opposed to simple travelers on the boat of history. The orchestra of our period, with its intricate songs and harmonies, is a demonstration of the human limit with respect to creation and obliteration. The Coda entreats us to be careful directors, directing this orchestra with intelligence, sympathy, and a resolute obligation to the benefit of all.

As we regard the call of the Coda, we become caretakers of an inheritance that reaches out past our singular lifetimes. The activities we take today resonate through the passageways of time, molding the fate of ages yet unborn. In this orchestra of presence, each note, each instrument, assumes a critical part in making a song that rises above the vaporous idea of our lives.

The Coda coaxes us to be stewards of the Earth, watchmen of equity, and draftsmen of a future where the reverberations of our activities resound with congruity instead of disunity. A call rises above the limits of country, doctrine, and belief system — a call that addresses the common goals of mankind. In the last examination, the Coda is a challenge to partake effectively in the continuous production of our aggregate predetermination, perceiving that the genuine proportion of our mankind lies not in what we have but rather in what we add to the more prominent orchestra of presence.

9.1 Summarize the key lessons learned from the exploration of nature's silent symphony.

The investigation of nature's quiet ensemble uncovers an embroidery woven by the many-sided strings of the regular world. As humankind digs into the mysteries of the climate, significant illustrations arise — examples that resound with biological importance as well as with significant ramifications for our aggregate presence. These examples reverberation through the ages, encouraging us to reevaluate our relationship with the Earth and rousing a more amicable and manageable conjunction.

The investigation of nature's quiet ensemble, first and foremost, highlights the interconnectedness of every living being. In the huge and multifaceted snare of biological systems, each organic entity, from the littlest microorganism to the biggest hunter, assumes an imperative part. The fragile equilibrium that supports life on Earth is a demonstration of the relationship of species, each contributing an exceptional note to the ensemble of nature. This interconnectedness isn't simply an organic peculiarity; it reaches out to the multifaceted dance of biological systems, environment designs, and the general wellbeing of the planet.

Perceiving this interconnectedness conveys significant ramifications for our stewardship of the climate. Human exercises, from deforestation to contamination, send swells through this interconnected web, influencing individual species as well as the whole outfit of life. The ensemble instructs us that our activities have outcomes that resonate through the biological system, influencing the prosperity of vegetation, fauna, and at last, mankind itself. Hence, the illustration learned is one of obligation — a call to careful concurrence and an acknowledgment of the effect every person and aggregate choice can have on the sensitive equilibrium of nature.

One more key illustration gathered from the investigation of nature's quiet orchestra is the significance of biodiversity. The variety of living things on Earth adds to the versatility and flexibility of environments.

Every species, with its novel qualities and variations, adds wealth to the ensemble, adding to the general wellbeing and usefulness of the regular world. Notwithstanding, human exercises, for example, territory obliteration and environmental change, undermine biodiversity at a disturbing rate.

The lessening tune of species all over the planet fills in as a distinct sign of the direness to secure and protect biodiversity. The illustration is clear: the deficiency of even a solitary animal groups can upset the congruity of the whole environment, prompting flowing impacts on different species and, at last, on the prosperity of humankind. Preservation endeavors and manageable practices arise as objectives considering this illustration, encouraging us to go about as stewards of biodiversity and gatekeepers of the heap life shapes that share this planet with us.

Moreover, the investigation of nature's quiet ensemble uncovers the significant versatility implanted in the regular world. Biological systems have developed over centuries, adjusting to changing ecological circumstances and tracking down clever answers for difficulties. The orchestra instructs us that versatility isn't just a quality of individual animal varieties yet a trait of whole environments. This flexibility is a wellspring of motivation as we face the ecological difficulties within recent memory, from environmental change to living space corruption.

Understanding and copying the versatility found in nature turns into a core value as we continued looking for maintainability. Impersonating nature's answers, embracing regenerative practices, and cultivating environments that can endure and recuperate from unsettling influences are vital parts of building a stronger and supportable future. The example here isn't just about alleviating the effects of human exercises yet gaining from nature's strength to co-make frameworks that can persevere and adjust even with progressing ecological changes.

All the while, the investigation of nature's quiet ensemble features the delicacy of environments notwithstanding human-instigated interruptions. The sped up speed of ecological change, driven by human exercises, presents exceptional difficulties to the fragile balance of nature. From the deficiency of living spaces to the presentation of intrusive species, our activities intensify the weakness of biological systems, driving them to the edge.

The example learned is a preventative one — an affirmation of the constraints of nature's strength even with anthropogenic tensions. It highlights the basic to address the underlying drivers of ecological debasement, underlining the requirement for maintainable practices, protection endeavors, and a key change in our relationship with the regular world. As overseers of the Earth, the onus is on humankind to proceed with caution, perceiving the delicacy of environments and endeavoring to limit our biological impression.

In addition, the investigation of nature's quiet ensemble causes to notice the repeating and regenerative cycles that support the working of environments.

From supplement cycles to the recurring pattern of seasons, nature works in a cadenced dance of reestablishment and resurrection. This repeating nature is a wellspring of motivation for economical works on, empowering us to adjust our exercises to the regular rhythms of the planet.

The illustration here is one of congruity and equilibrium — an update that economical arrangements should coordinate with, as opposed to disturb, the repeating cycles of nature. Whether in farming, asset the executives, or metropolitan preparation, the ensemble helps us to embrace roundabout economies and shut circle frameworks that emulate the regenerative examples saw as in the regular world. By adjusting our activities to the repetitive cycles of nature, we can make a more feasible and agreeable relationship with the Earth.

Besides, the investigation of nature's quiet ensemble welcomes examination on the inborn worth of the normal world. Past its instrumental utility for mankind, nature has inborn worth and magnificence that rises above human necessities. The different scenes, the bunch types of life, and the unpredictable exchange of components add to an ensemble of feel that improves the human experience.

The illustration learned is one of veneration and appreciation — a call to perceive the inborn worth of nature for the wellbeing of its own. This affirmation has significant ramifications for preservation morals, encouraging us to secure and safeguard regular spaces not only for their instrumental worth but rather for biodiversity, biological honesty, and the profound and stylish sustenance they give. The ensemble helps us to see nature as a wellspring of motivation, comfort, and marvel — a domain meriting our regard and insurance.

In the investigation of nature's quiet orchestra, an essential example unfurls with respect to the effect of environmental change on biological systems. The orchestra resonates with the reverberations of a planet in motion, as climbing temperatures, changing precipitation designs, and modified climatic circumstances challenge the versatility of both widely varied vegetation. The example learned is one of criticalness — an affirmation that environmental change is definitely not a far off danger however an impending emergency that requests quick and unequivocal activity.

Alleviating and adjusting to environmental change become goals woven into the texture of manageability. The orchestra instructs us that tending to environmental change isn't just about lessening ozone depleting substance discharges yet additionally about building versatile biological systems, cultivating economical practices, and embracing creative arrangements. The direness of the example urges us to change to a low-carbon future, where the ensemble of nature can keep on playing as one with the solidness of the environment.

As the investigation of nature's quiet ensemble unfurls, it becomes obvious that the safeguarding of regular living spaces is a key part in the preservation story. Biological systems, from rainforests to coral reefs, harbor an abundance of biodiversity and offer fundamental types of assistance, from carbon sequestration to water sanitization. The orchestra instructs us that the debasement and loss of these territories are a deficiency of organic variety as well as a danger to the mind boggling equilibrium of the whole planet.

The example learned is one of territory protection and rebuilding. Preservation endeavors should focus on the security of basic territories and the reclamation of corrupted biological systems. This illustration stresses the significance of making and keeping up with interconnected passageways that consider the development of species, working with hereditary variety and transformation. The orchestra highlights that the safeguarding of normal living spaces isn't an extravagance however a need for the prosperity of the whole planet.

All the while, the investigation of nature's quiet orchestra disentangles the significance of water as a central part of biological congruity. Freshwater biological systems, from waterways to wetlands, are essential to the orchestra of life, giving living spaces to endless species and supporting human networks. Notwithstanding, the orchestra additionally uncovers the weakness of water biological systems to contamination, over-extraction, and the effects of environmental change.

The example learned is one of water stewardship — an acknowledgment that the soundness of freshwater biological systems is naturally connected to the prosperity of the planet. Supportable water the executives rehearses, contamination counteraction, and the rebuilding of corrupted water bodies become fundamental parts of the preservation plan. The orchestra instructs us that defending water biological systems isn't just significant for biodiversity yet in addition for guaranteeing a manageable and impartial future for mankind.

In the investigation of nature's quiet orchestra, a strong illustration arises concerning the moral treatment of creatures. The orchestra reverberates with the variety of living things, each with its own characteristic worth and job in the biological system. Nonetheless, human exercises, from environment obliteration to poaching, compromise innumerable species, driving them to the edge of annihilation. The illustration learned is one of moral obligation — an affirmation that mankind bears an honest conviction to safeguard and regard the privileges of non-individuals.

Preservation endeavors should stretch out past charming megafauna to envelop all species, perceiving that each assumes a novel part in the ensemble of nature. The illustration urges us to embrace moral untamed life the travel industry, support preservation drives, and promoter for approaches that safeguard creatures from double-dealing and remorselessness. The ensemble instructs us that our moral treatment of creatures mirrors the profundity of our empathy and our obligation to coinciding agreeably with the assorted occupants of the Earth.

Besides, the investigation of nature's quiet ensemble welcomes reflection on the effect of human exercises on marine biological systems. Seas, with their tremendous regions and rich biodiversity, structure an essential piece of the worldwide ensemble of life. Notwithstanding, overfishing, contamination, and environmental change compromise the wellbeing of marine biological systems, imperiling the mind boggling balance that supports life underneath the waves.

The illustration learned is one of marine preservation — a call to shield the seas for the prosperity of both marine life and mankind. Supportable fishing rehearses, marine safeguarded regions, and endeavors to decrease plastic contamination become basic parts of this illustration. The ensemble instructs us that the wellbeing of marine environments is interlaced with the strength of the whole planet, and the safeguarding of seas is a common obligation that rises above public limits.

As the investigation of nature's quiet ensemble unfurls, it becomes obvious that native information holds significant examples for manageable living. Native people group, with their profound association with the land and conventional environmental information, have supported agreeable associations with nature for ages. The ensemble instructs us that native insight is a wellspring of motivation, offering bits of knowledge into supportable practices, biodiversity preservation, and the flexibility of environments.

The illustration learned is one of regard for native privileges and acknowledgment of the significance of coordinating customary information into contemporary preservation endeavors. Native people group, as stewards of different scenes, assume an imperative part in the protection of biodiversity and the support of environmental equilibrium. The orchestra urges us to team up with and gain from native people groups, cultivating a comprehensive way to deal with preservation that recognizes the insight implanted in their well established rehearses.

All in all, the investigation of nature's quiet orchestra unfurls a horde of illustrations that coax humankind to a more cognizant and amicable presence. From the interconnectedness of all living creatures to the earnest requirement for ecological stewardship, every illustration reverberates with the basic to reconsider our relationship with the Earth. The orchestra entreats us to be careful directors, directing the tune of presence with insight, empathy, and a significant regard for the mind boggling dance of nature. As we regard these illustrations, we become overseers of the climate as well as dynamic members in the continuous making of a maintainable and agreeable future for ages yet unborn.

9.2 Inspire readers to appreciate, respect, and actively contribute to preserving the delicate balance of the natural world.

In the tremendous embroidery of presence, the normal world unfurls as a magnum opus — a material painted with the tints of biodiversity, the songs of biological systems, and the perplexing dance of life. As we cross the scenes of our planet, it becomes basic to develop a significant appreciation for the sensitive equilibrium that supports this fabulous orchestra. This appreciation goes past a simple affirmation of nature's excellence; it is a call to see the interconnected strings that weave the texture of life and to perceive the inherent worth of each and every living being.

Think about the verdant woodlands, where daylight channels through the covering, sustaining a heap of plant animal varieties that, thusly, give shelter and food to innumerable animals. Picture the extensive seas, overflowing with life — from the glorious whales to the littlest microscopic fish — each assuming a special part in the sea-going expressive dance. Consider the tremendous deserts, where strong creatures have adjusted to outrageous circumstances, exhibiting the noteworthy variety of life's relentlessness. It is inside this variety and interconnectedness that the magnificence and meaning of the normal world become fully awake.

To see the value in the sensitive equilibrium of the normal world is to leave on an excursion of marvel and interest. It is a challenge to wonder about the complex variations of vegetation, from the disguise of a chameleon to the streamlined flawlessness of a bird's wing. It is an acknowledgment that each specie, regardless of how subtle, adds to the stupendous embroidery of biodiversity. The excellence lies not just in the energetic shades of a coral reef or the effortless trip of a butterfly yet in addition in the exchange of connections — hunter and prey, pollinator and blossom — that support the trap of life.

As we dive into the intricacy of environments, we uncover the interconnectedness that supports the working of our planet. The fragile equilibrium of nature is a demonstration of the reliance of species and the complex dance of energy and supplements. Think about the fundamental job of honey bees as pollinators, working with the propagation of blooming plants and guaranteeing the overflow of products of the soil. Ponder the complicated food networks that connect species in a fragile equilibrium, where the vanishing of one can send flowing impacts through the whole framework.

This association reaches out past the natural domain to the patterns of water, air, and soil that structure the groundwork of life. The downpour that sustains the dirt, the breeze that conveys seeds to new terrains, and the mind boggling dance of carbon through the air — this large number of components add to the orchestra of Earth. Perceiving this interconnectedness isn't just a question of logical seeing yet a call to see the value in the verse of nature, where each component has its impact in the fantastic story of presence.

Besides, an appreciation for the sensitive equilibrium of the normal world is indivisible from a profound regard for the characteristic worth of each and every living being. It is an acknowledgment that every animal categories has its own motivation, developing more than great many years to possess a particular specialty in the environment. From the grand hunters to the unassuming decomposers, every living being adds to the equilibrium and versatility of its territory. The ensemble of nature is a festival of variety, where each note, regardless of how delicate, enhances the general organization.

This regard for characteristic worth stretches out to the affirmation that nature has innate worth past its utility to mankind. It is a call to move past survey the normal world exclusively from the perspective of asset extraction and financial increase. Nature, in the entirety of its structures, has an option to exist and flourish, free of its instrumental worth to people. A tree in a woodland, a frog in a lake, a mountain range — each merits regard and security, for the administrations it gives as well as to its innate right to exist as a piece of the interconnected entirety.

In developing an appreciation and regard for the fragile equilibrium of the regular world, it becomes occupant upon us to perceive our job as stewards of the Earth. Mankind, with its ability for information and organization, is particularly situated to either upset or fit with the complex rhythms of nature. Our decisions as people and social orders echo through the biological systems of our planet, affecting the prosperity of greenery, fauna, and at last, our own species.

Protecting the sensitive equilibrium of the normal world is definitely not a theoretical idea yet a substantial obligation that requires smart and purposeful activity. It is an acknowledgment that our activities, from the littlest everyday decisions to the more fabulous choices that shape strategies, have results that reverberation through the trap of life. Consider the effect of deforestation on the environments of innumerable species or the contamination that debases air and water quality, jeopardizing biological systems and human wellbeing the same. The sensitive equilibrium is effectively disturbed, and our activities assume a significant part in either keeping up with or weakening it.

The protection of the sensitive equilibrium of the normal world starts with a guarantee to manageable practices in each feature of life. It includes reconsidering our utilization designs, lessening waste, and embracing rehearses that limit our biological impression. From energy utilization to food decisions, every choice can add to a more supportable and amicable relationship with the climate. This isn't a call for plainness however a challenge to adjust our ways of life to the regenerative limit of the planet, guaranteeing that people in the future acquire a world wealthy in biodiversity and environmental imperativeness.

Besides, saving the fragile equilibrium requires a pledge to preservation and living space security. It includes defending regular spaces, from flawless wild regions to metropolitan green spaces, perceiving their significance for biodiversity, diversion, and the prosperity of networks. Protection endeavors should stretch out past magnetic species to include whole biological systems, recognizing that the soundness of the planet depends on the variety and strength of natural surroundings. This requires supporting and upholding for arrangements and drives that focus on the protection of normal spaces, perceiving their inborn worth and the administrations they give to mankind.

The sensitive equilibrium of the regular world is personally connected to the worldwide test of environmental change. The change of environment designs, driven by human exercises like consuming petroleum derivatives and deforestation, represents a significant danger to biological systems and biodiversity. Saving the sensitive equilibrium requires a coordinated work to relieve and adjust to environmental change. This includes progressing to environmentally friendly power sources, safeguarding and reestablishing carbon-sequestering biological systems like woods and wetlands, and pushing for strategies that address the underlying drivers of environmental change. The orchestra of nature, unpredictably associated with environment solidness, relies upon our capacity to check ozone harming substance emanations and encourage versatility notwithstanding continuous ecological changes.

Notwithstanding individual and aggregate activities, protecting the sensitive equilibrium of the normal world requires a change in perspective in cultural qualities and needs. It requires rethinking achievement not exclusively in financial terms but rather as far as natural maintainability and the prosperity of every single living being. The ensemble instructs us that the quest for interminable development to the detriment of the climate is unreasonable and eventually pointless. We should embrace models of improvement that focus on biological trustworthiness, social value, and the conservation of biodiversity.

Training turns into a strong instrument in this extraordinary excursion. Cultivating a comprehension of the sensitive equilibrium between the regular world, its interconnectedness, and the significance of biodiversity can impart a feeling of obligation and organization in people. Instruction enables individuals to go with informed decisions, advocate for maintainable practices, and add to the more extensive cultural shift towards ecological stewardship. It is an interest from now on, sustaining an age that values the magnificence of nature as well as effectively attempts to protect it.

Moreover, a vital part of protecting the fragile equilibrium lies in cultivating a feeling of association and connection with the regular world. It includes reconnecting with nature, whether through outside encounters, ecological schooling, or essentially investing energy in green spaces. This reconnection isn't simply a way to get away from the burdens of present day life however a major change in context — an acknowledgment that we are a piece of, not separated from, the many-sided snare of life.

The ensemble welcomes us to encounter the magnificence of a dawn, the quietness of a timberland, and the stunning variety of life, developing a feeling of obligation and love for the planet that supports us.

Additionally, the conservation of the fragile equilibrium requires support for strategies that reflect natural awareness and advance maintainability. It includes considering policymakers responsible for choices that influence the normal world and upholding for guidelines that focus on protection, environment activity, and the prosperity of biological systems. Community commitment, from taking part in nearby ecological drives to supporting worldwide endeavors, turns into an essential road for people to add to the more extensive development for natural safeguarding.

As we leave on the excursion to protect the fragile equilibrium of the normal world, it is fundamental to recognize that this is definitely not a singular undertaking. The ensemble of nature requires an aggregate exertion — an amicable cooperation between people, networks, legislatures, and global associations. The difficulties we face, from biodiversity misfortune to environment.

9.3 Provide practical steps and resources for individuals to engage in conservation efforts.

Setting out on the excursion of protection isn't saved for ecological specialists or those with broad assets; it is an aggregate liability that each individual can add to. As the sensitive equilibrium of the regular world remains in a critical state, making functional strides towards protection turns out to be more significant than any other time in recent memory. Whether you dwell in a metropolitan place or a provincial local area, there are different reasonable measures and assets accessible for people to participate in protection endeavors and have a significant effect on the climate effectively.

1. **Instruct Yourself As well as other people:**

   A principal move toward drawing in with preservation endeavors is to gain information about ecological issues, biodiversity, and the nearby environments. Understanding the difficulties looked by the climate furnishes people with the data expected to pursue informed choices. There are various internet based assets, narratives, and instructive stages that give significant bits of knowledge into natural issues. Drives like web-based courses, online classes, and studios co-ordinated by natural associations offer available roads for learning and remaining informed.

As well as teaching yourself, spreading mindfulness among family, companions, and local area individuals is a strong method for intensifying the effect of protection endeavors.

Share data about nearby ecological issues, the significance of biodiversity, and reasonable tips for practical living. Virtual entertainment stages, local area occasions, and instructive studios are compelling channels for scattering data and encouraging an aggregate feeling of obligation.

2. **Lessen, Reuse, and Reuse:**

   Quite possibly of the most pragmatic and significant step people can take in their regular routines is to embrace the mantra of "lessen, reuse, and reuse." Diminishing utilization limits the interest for assets and decreases the natural impression. Picking reusable items, for example, water bottles, shopping packs, and holders, mitigates the effect of single-use plastics. Reusing materials like paper, glass, and plastics redirects squander from landfills, rationing assets and diminishing contamination.

   Nearby reusing projects and offices frequently give rules on the most proficient method to appropriately sort and reuse materials. Numerous people group likewise arrange assortment occasions for electronic waste, perilous materials, and different things that require specific reusing processes. Being aware of individual utilization and waste age is a substantial way for people to add to preservation consistently.

3. **Preserve Water:**

   Water is a limited asset, and its preservation is indispensable to keeping up with the fragile equilibrium of biological systems. People can assume a part in water protection through basic yet significant practices. Fixing spills, utilizing water-effective apparatuses, and consolidating water-saving advancements, like low-stream fixtures and showerheads, add to decreasing water utilization.

   Also, finishing decisions can essentially influence water use. Picking local and dry spell safe plants decreases the requirement for unnecessary watering. Gathering water for garden water system is another manageable practice that preserves water assets. Numerous districts and natural associations offer assets and rules for water preservation, enabling people to pursue informed decisions in their regular routines.

4. **Support Feasible Practices in Farming:**

   The horticultural area assumes an essential part in biodiversity and biological system wellbeing. People can uphold feasible farming by going with informed decisions about the food they eat. Picking privately obtained, natural, and economically created food advances rehearses that focus on soil wellbeing, biodiversity, and decreased substance inputs.

   Drawing in with local area upheld horticulture (CSA) projects or neighborhood ranchers' business sectors is a down to earth method for supporting practical farming while at the same time associating with nearby food makers. Moreover, developing a little nursery at home, whether in a terrace or on an overhang, permits people to encounter the delights of developing their own food while advancing feasible practices.

5. **Take part in Resident Science Drives:**
Resident science programs give an open door to people to add to logical exploration and protection endeavors effectively. Numerous associations and research organizations team up with residents to gather information on different ecological peculiarities, from bird movement examples to water quality appraisals. Taking part in such drives permits people to contribute significant information while acquiring a more profound comprehension of neighborhood environments.

Online stages and versatile applications frequently work with resident science support, making it open to a more extensive crowd. Projects like eBird, iNaturalist, and Globe Around evening time connect with people in reporting biodiversity, following species disseminations, and observing light contamination. By taking part in resident science drives, people become fundamental supporters of logical information and protection.

6. **Support and Draw in with Preservation Associations:**
Ecological and preservation associations assume an imperative part in safeguarding biodiversity and normal natural surroundings. People can effectively uphold these associations by becoming individuals, volunteers, or givers. Numerous associations coordinate local area occasions, tree establishing drives, and environment rebuilding projects that give active open doors to people to add to protection endeavors.

Notwithstanding immediate commitment, people can remain educated about the work regarding preservation associations and backer for strategies that advance natural security. Sharing data about effective preservation projects, supporting petitions, and drawing in with neighborhood and public policymakers add to a more extensive development for natural protection.

7. **Encourage Supportable Travel Practices:**
For the individuals who appreciate travel, taking on maintainable practices can limit the natural effect of the travel industry. Picking eco-accommodating facilities, supporting neighborhood organizations, and deciding on low-influence transportation strategies, for example, trekking or strolling, add to dependable the travel industry. Numerous objections have ecotourism drives that focus on preservation and local area commitment.

Moreover, people can counterbalance their carbon impression by supporting reforestation activities or putting resources into carbon offset programs. Going with a mentality of ecological stewardship guarantees that people can partake in the magnificence of different environments without undermining their honesty.

8. **Engage in Neighborhood Protection Activities:**

Neighborhood protection activities and local area drives give open doors to people to straightforwardly add to the prosperity of their environmental factors. Whether partaking in tree establishing occasions, tidying up nearby stops, or participating in living space reclamation projects, these involved exercises fortify the association among people and their neighborhood biological systems.

Numerous regions and ecological associations arrange volunteer open doors and protection projects. Joining nearby ecological gatherings or nature clubs gives a stage to people to team up with similar local area individuals, share encounters, and effectively add to the protection of neighborhood biodiversity.

9. **Pick Practical Energy Choices:**

The energy area altogether impacts the strength of the climate. Picking practical energy choices is a pivotal move toward decreasing fossil fuel byproducts and moderating the effects of environmental change. People can investigate environmentally friendly power sources, for example, sun based or wind power for their homes. Numerous areas offer motivators, sponsorships, or supporting choices to empower the reception of sustainable power advancements.

Moreover, supporting strategies and drives that advance clean energy at neighborhood, public, and worldwide levels is a method for pushing for a change to maintainable energy rehearses. Remaining informed about energy-effective advances and carrying out them in day to day existence adds to diminishing the carbon impression related with energy utilization.

10. **Practice Capable Untamed life Review:**

Valuing untamed life in their normal natural surroundings is an honor that accompanies an obligation to limit unsettling influence and guarantee the prosperity of the species noticed. Whether birdwatching, climbing, or taking part in natural life visits, people can rehearse capable natural life seeing by complying with moral rules.

Keeping a conscious separation, keeping away from direct impedance with natural life, and following assigned trails add to limiting human effect. Numerous associations give assets on capable untamed life seeing works on, guaranteeing that people can partake in nature's marvels without compromising the wellbeing and conduct of the species they experience.

11. **Advocate for Preservation Strategies:**

People have the ability to impact strategy choices that influence the climate. Support for preservation strategies at the neighborhood, public, and worldwide levels is a proactive move toward making a lawful system that focuses on natural insurance. Drawing in with chose authorities, partaking in formal reviews, and supporting ecological missions enhance the aggregate voice for protection.

Remaining informed about proposed strategies, grasping their suggestions, and speaking with policymakers guarantee that people can add to the improvement of regulation that lines up with protection objectives. Joining or supporting ecological backing bunches gives a stage to people to team up with similar promoters and all things considered impact strategy choices.

12. **Energize Manageable Practices in Your People group:**

People can have a critical effect by advancing manageable practices inside their networks. Whether through sorting out local area tidy up occasions, pushing for reusing projects, or supporting nearby natural drives, people can move aggregate activity. Showing others how its done, sharing information, and encouraging a feeling of local area commitment make a far reaching influence that stretches out past individual endeavors.

Empowering neighborhood organizations to embrace feasible works on, supporting eco-accommodating drives, and teaming up with local area pioneers add to the production of a culture that values natural protection. Local area based arrangements frequently have a more prompt and noticeable effect, cultivating a feeling of satisfaction and shared liability.

Taking part in protection endeavors is a source of inspiration that rises above individual activities — it's an aggregate liability woven into the texture of our interconnected world. Every individual, paying little heed to foundation or ability, has the ability to make significant commitments toward the safeguarding of the climate. As we explore a world wrestling with natural difficulties, viable advances and a pledge to manageability can enhance the effect of individual endeavors. Here, we investigate a far reaching guide, offering bits of knowledge and assets for people to take part in preservation and become stewards of the planet effectively.

1. **Cultivate Ecological Mindfulness:**
   The groundwork of compelling preservation endeavors lies in encouraging ecological mindfulness. People can begin by instructing themselves about ecological issues, environmental change, and the effect of human exercises on biological systems. Open assets, including narratives, books, and online stages, offer significant bits of knowledge into the complexities of natural difficulties. By understanding the issues, people can more readily value the earnestness of preservation and settle on informed decisions in their regular routines.
   Spreading attention to companions, family, and networks is similarly indispensable. Taking part in discussions about natural issues, sharing data via web-based entertainment, and taking an interest in neighborhood conversations add to an aggregate comprehension of the difficulties within reach. Informed people can act as impetuses for more extensive change, making a gradually expanding influence that broadens the span of protection endeavors.

2. **Practice Supportable Utilization:**

   People apply a significant impact through their ordinary utilization decisions. Embracing supportable practices in utilization is a substantial method for diminishing natural effect. This incorporates deciding on items with negligible bundling, picking energy-proficient machines, and supporting organizations with ecologically cognizant practices. Cognizant industrialism limits squander as well as urges organizations to take on feasible practices.

   Moreover, lessening meat utilization and integrating plant-based food varieties into diets can add to bringing down the natural impression related with farming. Economical food decisions, like supporting neighborhood ranchers and picking occasional produce, line up with preservation objectives by advancing biodiversity and diminishing the carbon impression related with food creation.

3. **Lessen, Reuse, Reuse:**

   The immortal mantra of "decrease, reuse, reuse" stays a foundation of protection endeavors. People can limit squander by deliberately lessening their utilization of single-use things and embracing reusable other options. Putting resources into solid items, for example, reusable water bottles, shopping packs, and holders, fundamentally decreases how much plastic waste entering landfills and biological systems.

   Legitimate reusing rehearses likewise assume a significant part. Really getting to know nearby reusing rules, arranging materials accurately, and taking part in reusing programs add to the effective administration of waste. Numerous people group put together electronic waste reusing occasions, giving roads to dependable removal of things like old gadgets.

4. **Preserve Energy:**

   Tending to the worldwide test of environmental change requires an emphasis on energy preservation. People can contribute by embracing energy-effective practices in their homes. Straightforward advances, for example, switching out lights when not being used, turning off hardware, and utilizing energy-effective machines altogether decrease power utilization.

   Investigating environmentally friendly power choices for homes, like sunlight based chargers or wind turbines, lines up with a practical energy future. Numerous areas offer motivating forces and funding choices to help the reception of environmentally friendly power advances. Moreover, pushing for and supporting approaches that elevate the progress to clean energy at the local area and public levels adds to more extensive preservation objectives.

5. **Practice Capable Water Use:**

   Water shortage is a squeezing worldwide concern, and people can assume a part in water protection through careful practices. Fixing spills, utilizing water-productive apparatuses, and consolidating water-saving innovations, like low-stream spigots and showerheads, add to diminishing water utilization. Saving water in day to day exercises, like washing dishes or watering plants, guarantees capable use.

Finishing decisions additionally influence water use. Choosing local plants and carrying out water gathering frameworks for garden water system add to maintainable water the executives. Numerous people group give assets and rules to water protection, engaging people to have a constructive outcome on nearby water environments.

6. **Support Preservation Associations:**

Preservation associations assume a critical part in safeguarding biodiversity and normal environments. People can effectively uphold these associations by becoming individuals, volunteers, or givers. Numerous preservation bunches arrange local area occasions, tree establishing drives, and living space rebuilding projects that give active open doors to people to add to protection endeavors.

Notwithstanding immediate commitment, remaining educated about the work regarding preservation associations and pushing for arrangements that advance ecological insurance is pivotal. Supporting and partaking in natural life protection projects, reforestation drives, and living space safeguarding endeavors add to the more extensive development for ecological preservation.

7. **Engage in Resident Science:**

Resident science drives offer a one of a kind chance for people to add to logical examination and protection endeavors effectively. Numerous associations and research establishments team up with residents to gather information on different ecological peculiarities, from bird movement examples to water quality evaluations. Partaking in resident science projects permits people to contribute important information while acquiring a more profound comprehension of nearby biological systems.

Online stages and versatile applications work with resident science cooperation, making it open to a more extensive crowd. Projects like eBird, iNaturalist, and Zooniverse connect with people in recording biodiversity, following species disseminations, and adding to logical information. By taking part in resident science drives, people become basic supporters of understanding and monitoring the regular world.

8. **Support Manageable Farming:**

Individuals decisions with respect to food have huge ramifications for the climate. Supporting economical horticulture includes pursuing informed decisions about the food devoured. Selecting privately obtained, natural, and reasonably delivered food advances rehearses that focus on soil wellbeing, biodiversity, and diminished substance inputs.

Drawing in with local area upheld horticulture (CSA) projects or nearby ranchers' business sectors is a reasonable method for supporting manageable farming while at the same time interfacing with neighborhood food makers.

Furthermore, developing a little nursery at home, whether in a patio or on an overhang, permits people to encounter the delights of developing their own food while advancing economical practices.

9. **Take part in Manageable Travel Practices:**

   For the people who appreciate travel, embracing economical practices can limit the natural effect of the travel industry. Picking eco-accommodating facilities, supporting nearby organizations, and selecting low-influence transportation strategies, for example, trekking or strolling, add to dependable the travel industry. Numerous objections have ecotourism drives that focus on protection and local area commitment.

   Moreover, people can balance their carbon impression by supporting reforestation undertakings or putting resources into carbon offset programs. Going with a mentality of ecological stewardship guarantees that people can partake in the magnificence of different biological systems without undermining their uprightness.

10. **Partake in Nearby Preservation Undertakings:**

    Neighborhood preservation activities and local area drives give open doors to people to straightforwardly add to the prosperity of their environmental factors. Whether taking part in tree establishing occasions, tidying up neighborhood stops, or participating in environment rebuilding projects, these active exercises reinforce the association among people and their nearby biological systems.

    Numerous districts and natural associations put together worker open doors and protection projects. Joining nearby ecological gatherings or nature clubs gives a stage to people to team up with similar local area individuals, share encounters, and effectively add to the protection of neighborhood biodiversity.

11. **Pick Economical Energy Choices:**

    The energy area fundamentally impacts the strength of the climate. Picking manageable energy choices is a pivotal move toward decreasing fossil fuel byproducts and relieving the effects of environmental change. People can investigate sustainable power sources, for example, sunlight based or wind power for their homes. Numerous locales offer motivations, appropriations, or funding choices to support the reception of environmentally friendly power innovations.

    Moreover, supporting strategies and drives that advance clean energy at nearby, public, and worldwide levels is a method for upholding for a change to economical energy rehearses. Remaining informed about energy-effective advancements and carrying out them in day to day existence adds to lessening the carbon impression related with energy utilization.

12. **Advocate for Protection Strategies:**

    People have the ability to impact strategy choices that influence the climate. Promotion for preservation strategies at the neighborhood, public, and worldwide levels is a proactive move toward making a lawful system that focuses on ecological insurance. Drawing in with chose authorities, partaking in formal reviews, and supporting ecological missions enhance the aggregate voice for preservation.

Remaining informed about proposed arrangements, grasping their suggestions, and speaking with policymakers guarantee that people can add to the improvement of regulation that lines up with protection objectives. Joining or supporting natural promotion bunches gives a stage to people to team up with similar backers and by and large impact strategy choices.

13. **Energize Feasible Practices in Your People group:** People can have a critical effect by advancing feasible practices inside their networks. Whether through putting together local area tidy up occasions, pushing for reusing projects, or supporting nearby natural drives, people can motivate aggregate activity. Showing others how its done, sharing information, and cultivating a feeling of local area commitment make a gradually expanding influence that stretches out past individual endeavors.

Empowering neighborhood organizations to take on reasonable works on, supporting eco-accommodating drives, and teaming up with local area pioneers add to the formation of a culture that values natural protection. Local area based arrangements frequently have a more prompt and noticeable effect, encouraging a feeling of satisfaction and shared liability.

www.ingramcontent.com/pod-product-compliance
Lightning Source LLC
LaVergne TN
LVHW020817200726
843506LV00009B/1086